THE UNOFFICIAL NURSE'S HANDBOOK

THE UNOFFICIAL NURSE'S HANDBOOK

by Nina Schroeder, R.N.
with Richard Mintzer

Produced by Ultra Communications, Inc.

A PLUME BOOK

NEW AMERICAN LIBRARY

A DIVISION OF PENGUIN BOOKS USA INC., NEW YORK
PUBLISHED IN CANADA BY
PENGUIN BOOKS CANADA LIMITED, MARKHAM, ONTARIO

Copyright © 1986 by Ultra Communications, Inc.

Additional contributions by Susan Netter

Illustrations by Joel Weissman

PLUME TRADEMARK REG. U.S. PAT. OFF. AND FOREIGN COUNTRIES
REG. TRADEMARK—MARCA REGISTRADA
HECHO EN BRATTLEBORO, VT., U.S.A.

SIGNET, SIGNET CLASSIC, MENTOR, ONYX, PLUME, MERIDIAN and
NAL BOOKS are published *in the United States* by New American Library,
a division of Penguin Books USA Inc., 1633 Broadway, New York, New York
10019, *in Canada* by Penguin Books Canada Limited, 2801 John Street,
Markham, Ontario L3R 1B4.

Library of Congress Cataloging-in-Publication Data

Schroeder, Nina.
  The unofficial nurse's handbook.

  1. Nursing—Anecdotes, facetiae, satire, etc.
2. Nurses—Anecdotes, facetiae, satire, etc.
I. Mintzer, Richard. II. Title.
RT42.S37   1986   610.73   86-12619
ISBN 0-452-25899-5

First Printing, November, 1986
        8   9   10   11

PRINTED IN THE UNITED STATES OF AMERICA

Acknowledgments

I'd like to thank Ronnie Linder, a retired R.N. with great stories to tell, Rosemary Sciarrino, a most enthusiastic and helpful R.N., Greg Imballis, R.N., Cathy Valez, R.N., Tom Padovano for some ninth-inning pinch-hit lines, Kathi Lipschitz for proofing while pregnant, Dave Lipschitz for computer madness, Jerry Mintzer for support, Carol Friedfel for help and patience, Muriel Mintzer for working at Tiffany's, and a couple of tireless, hard-working round-the-clock computers.

"And Grandma, don't worry. Just because I took the facts of nursing, made them funny, and picked on some hospital personnel here and there doesn't mean they won't let me in a hospital . . . I hope."

Rich Mintzer

Contents

4 Specialties of the Hospital 55

5 How to Succeed in a Hospital Without Even Crying 77

6 The Personal

Nurse 1. A person trained to care for the sick, elderly, or disabled despite the supervision of a physician. 2. Usually resides in overcrowded quarters with other nurses . . . *see:*   Ghetto. 3. Someone who believes in a seventy-five-hour work week. (The reason for this has yet to be determined.)

CHAPTER ONE

Yes, Even You Can Be a Nurse

"I Want to Be a Nurse"

Remember, when you were a kid, and the doctor gave you a shot that made you cry, how the nurse took you aside and made you feel better? Remember when you were growing up, how the worldwide lifesaving exploits and fabulous adventures of Cherry Ames made you fantasize what it might be like to be in her shoes? Remember all those war movies where the sole nurse on the scene had her pick of all the handsome doctors—and the grateful wounded patients as well?

These are merely a few reasons why you may be among the millions who look themselves in the mirror and say, "I want to be a nurse." And there are many other reasons. Perhaps all your life you willingly took care of dolls, plants, pets, baby brother and sister; waited on Mommy and Daddy when they were sick or hung over; ran to help injured classmates or boyfriends; spent your allowance on Band-Aids, aspirin, and chicken soup; or hid a poor orphan child in your room for a year. You may even have said to yourself way back then, "I want to be a nurse."

Perhaps having control over people from all social classes and income levels appeals to you. The prospect of having executives (who'd think nothing of putting you on hold for forty minutes) suddenly call desperately for a bedpan may be reason enough for saying, "I want to be a nurse."

It may be the opportunity to work closely with doctors, to see firsthand how skilled some are at their craft—and catch others with their Hippocratic oaths down—that leads you to say, "I want to be a nurse."

But can you do it? Do you really like sick people? Naked people? Grumpy people? Egomaniacs? Doctors? (The last two may be redundant.) How do you feel about stuff that goes into and comes out of people? Flowers? Eight-hour workdays that feel like twelve? Never seeing real food again? Well, before you utter those six fateful words, "I want to be a nurse," it's time to turn the page and see if you truly are . . . nurse material.

ENTRANCE EXAM
A Test to Determine If You Have What It Takes to Become a Nurse

1. In all white you look:

   (A) Clean and dignified.
   (B) Like an ice cream salesperson.
   (C) Like a beached whale.

2. The sight of blood makes you:

   (A) Thirsty.
   (B) Run to the bathroom and gag.
   (C) Run and get your always-handy first-aid kit.

3. Your idea of an average working day is:

   (A) 8 hours.
   (B) 10 hours.
   (C) 24 hours.

4. The term "O.R." stands for:

(A) Oral Roberts.
(B) Operating Room.
(C) Oral retentive.

5. You fantasize being a part of:

(a) St. Elsewhere.
(B) The A-Team.
(C) Star Search.

6. If the head nurse asked you to name all the patients on the floor, you would reply:

(A) "Why? They already have names."
(B) "Would you like that to be last name first, or first name first?"
(C) "I'll gladly return with that information after a short break."

7. An EKG monitor:

(A) Measures heart activity.
(B) Plays video cassettes.
(C) Guards the EKG.

8. When you hear the term "hospital," the first thing that comes to mind is:

(A) Good health care.
(B) Lousy food.
(C) Horror films.

9. One of your most common fantasies is:

(A) Heading the nursing staff of New York Medical Center.
(B) Being Head Nurse on *General Hospital*.
(C) Having three weeks' vacation in Hawaii.

10. To you, the term "rotation" means:

(A) Watching your favorite Madonna album spin on the stereo.
(B) Alternating shifts so as never to establish a social life, or to eliminate any you might have.
(C) The correct manner in which to move a patient to change his bedding.

11. In school you:

    (A) Enjoyed dissecting frogs.
    (B) Preferred assisting in the dissecting of frogs.
    (C) Attempted to reassemble previously dissected frogs.

12. Let's word associate—"dressing":

    (A) Salad.
    (B) Bandage.
    (C) Undressing.

13. Hospital gowns are designed to be:

    (A) Open in the back.
    (B) Open in the front.
    (C) Flammable.

14. In your leisure time you enjoy:

    (A) Charity work.
    (B) Boxing matches.
    (C) Dissecting frogs.

15. If you could have three wishes they would be:

(A) Peace on earth, an end to world hunger and suffering, and good health and happiness for everyone.

(B) An end to world hunger and suffering, eight more hours in a day, and some extra money for the essentials in life.

(C) Mel Gibson, Don Johnson, and two weeks in the Caribbean.

Answer Key

1. (A) 4 (B) 0 (C) 0
2. (A) 0 (B) 0 (C) 4
3. (A) 0 (B) 2 (C) 3
4. (A) 0 (B) 2 (C) 3
5. (A) 3 (B) 2 (C) 0 (The A-Team could use a psychiatric nurse.)
6. (A) 0 (B) 3 (C) 1
7. (A) 4 (B) 0 (C) 0
8. (A) 3 (B) 1 (C) 1
9. (A) 4 (B) 0 (C) 1 (It's nice to think about Hawaii now and then, even if you can't afford it.)
10. (A) 1 (B) 4 (C) 0
11. (A) 0 (B) 4 (C) 0
12. (A) 1 (B) 3 (C) 1
13. (A) 4 (B) 0 (C) 0
14. (A) 4 (B) 0 (C) 1
15. (A) 1 (B) 3 (C) 2 ("A" fits if you're up for Miss America. As for "C," there's nothing wrong with thinking about the Caribbean now and then, even if you can't afford it.)

Totals

48–53 Florence Nightingale has nothing on you. Go for it!

41–47 You have strong "Save the World" tendencies. Face it, you should pursue the big "R.N." as a career.

33–40 You might make it as a candy striper.

26–32 You could work in the hospital gift shop.

0–25 You're a danger to the safety of a hospital, clinic, or even a surgical supply store.

The Top Ten Reasons for Becoming a Nurse

1. To prove once and for all that you *do* have a strong stomach.
2. You have an overwhelming urge to humiliate doctors—or marry them.
3. To prove to everyone that an "A+" in high school chemistry *does* mean something, after all.
4. White is *your* color.
5. You blew your chance to become a nun—at age fourteen.
6. You're a natural-born "night person."
7. You still love to "assist" when playing doctor.
8. You went to visit a friend in the hospital—and never left.
9. You couldn't get an acting role on *St. Elsewhere,* so you opted for the real thing.
10. You flunked out of ballet school.

The Nine-Year-Old Nurse

How to Spot a Future Nurse in the Family

Does *your* nine-year-old show any of these telltale signs? Does she or he:

1. Prefer cardigan sweaters, keep her white shoes spotless, and have frequent urges to put cupcakes on her head?

2. Spend an inordinate amount of time taking her Cabbage Patch doll's "temp."?
3. Show an abnormal enthusiasm for changing sheets and draperies?
4. Spend free time putting aspirin in paper cups?
5. Stand by Daddy's side on Thanksgiving, handing him the utensils for carving the turkey, and preferring to administer the dressing after carving rather than eat it?
6. Thoroughly enjoy listening to her grandparents complaining?

7. Try to rewrap mummies during class trips to museums?
8. Like to take other children's blood pressure before and after recess?
9. Only show interest in sporting events when someone is injured on the field?
10. Insist his GI Joe doll is a medic?

The Nurse's Code
(Thank Hippocrates It's Not an Oath!)

The nurse hereby:

1. Agrees to safeguard a patient's privacy, and thus refrain from turning someone's personal life into gossip, grist for *National Enquirer* cover stories, or scripts for afternoon soaps.
2. Agrees to safeguard a patient when his/her care is threatened. This includes warding off Peeping Toms, unwanted family members, medical students, hospital tours, reporters, the staff of *Late Night with David Letterman,* ambulance-chasing lawyers, or terrorists who may be seeking your patient, bomb in hand.
3. Is fully prepared to ingest, digest, reject, or eject whatever newfangled substances Igor and the other lab technicians have dreamed up before administering them to patients. The same goes for hospital food.
4. Refuses to give personal endorsements for the advertising, promotion, or sale of commercial products such as the new line of Nightingale Nighties, Cabbage Patch doll stethoscopes, Doggie Mittens called "Gauze for Paws," Surgical Swimwear, or any of the Supernurse Activewear sporting the giant R.N. (this includes the cape, hat, gloves, goggles, and dickey).
5. Promises to follow the orders of the physician for the patient's care—at least while the physician is present.

Is Florence a City in Italy?
A Quiz on the First Lady of Nursing

1. Florence is:

(A) A name for girls with an unfortunate penchant for peanut butter and cheese puffs.
(B) A kind of neon light.
(C) A city in Italy.

2. From her habit of walking the halls of the hospital at night, British soldiers nicknamed her:

(A) "Bigfoot."
(B) "The lady with the lamp."
(C) "The lady with insomnia."

3. In 1854 Great Britain:

(A) Was Prussia.
(B) Asked Florence to take charge of nursing in the Crimean War.
(C) Declared war on Germany, Italy, and Utah (primarily to see Florence in action).

4. In 1856 Florence Nightingale founded:

(A) The Nite Owl Home for Wayward Nurses.
(B) Radio City Music Hall, where she wowed audiences seven nights a week.
(C) Albert Einstein Medical Center.

5. In the hospitals, Florence Nightingale began classes to teach convalescent soldiers:

(A) To read and write.
(B) To drink hot tea with lemon through a straw—and like it.
(C) To keep their hands to themselves.

6. Florence Nightingale was chiefly noted for introducing:

(A) Sanitary methods of nursing in wartime.
(B) Ways of nursing sanitation workers in peacetime.
(C) Black coffee to the nursing world.

"Who's the Nurse?": A Cheer

- Who's the nurse who started it all?   FLORENCE! FLORENCE!

- Who's the nurse who got the medals?   FLORENCE! FLORENCE!

- Who's the nurse who had no one to rotate with?   FLORENCE! FLORENCE!

- Who's the nurse who coined the phrase "Are we comfy"?   FLORENCE! FLORENCE!

- Who's the nurse who never faced a temperamental vending machine on her shift?   FLORENCE! FLORENCE!

- Who's the nurse so wonderfully skilled that countries would start wars just to see her in action?   FLORENCE! FLORENCE!

- Who's the nurse who could have made the cover of *People* magazine?   FLORENCE! FLORENCE!

- Who's this nurse named FLORENCE, and is she available for a night shift?   (cartwheels)

We'll Be Back After This Brief Coffee Break

Q: What's the difference between single nurses and married nurses?

A: Single nurses can date a wide variety of handsome residents and doctors from the hospital. Married nurses could have done the same thing, but were smart enough to know better.

Q: Why do surgeons wear the same shoes for ten years?

A: They have to because they're the only shoes their mothers haven't bronzed.

HOW TO GET YOUR NURSING LICENSE

1. Spend twenty-seven days and nights locked in seclusion studying for your nursing boards.

2. Develop Mafia connections.

3. Find a nurse who looks exactly like you, buy her license, and assume her identity.

4. Take the nursing boards in a foreign country.

A MYTH ABOUT NURSES

Nurses make terrific lovers, because they are such warm people and know so much about the human body.

The truth:

Nurses make terrific lovers, because they are such warm people and know so much about the human body.

CHAPTER TWO

NURSING SCHOOL, or "Do I Really Have a Strong Stomach?"

If the Cap Fits, Wear It

How to Choose a Nursing School

Once you've decided that you'd rather be a nurse than a nun, your next step is choosing a school at which to learn the basics—and then some. One might choose a college with a prestigious nursing program. On the other hand, one might choose a college because it has a losing, injury-prone football team on which to practice. The other alternative is a *bona fide* nursing school. Here the choice deals with reputation, scope of the program, location, and the most important element of all— The Nursing School Cap.

Despite the well-known fact that few working nurses wear caps any longer, nursing school caps become, and remain, a part of you until graduation. Thus the cap should and will hold precedence in your ultimate schooling decision.

CAPS: WHAT ARE THEY?
The styles and varieties of cap facing the career nurse are numerous, ranging from the stereotypical TV nursing cap to that resembling the Flying Nun's. Where one institution may sport the muffin cap, resembling a paper cup, another may feature

a cap in the design of a folded paper napkin. (If you're a sports fan, you may even find one similar to a baseball cap.)

CAP BANDS AND YOU

As opposed to school marching bands, cap bands are the colored bands that adorn the white cap you've so painstakingly chosen. Finding "your" color may be the catalyst for making your decision. As to cap bands, caps, and, ultimately, nursing schools, here's where you learn to be careful and avoid the napkin-shaped cap, whose band is likely to resemble a napkin ring. (This can lead to unpleasant dinner accidents.)

The answer to every aspiring nurse's cap-quandary may lie in the shape of her head and her hairstyle. Many fledgling nurses find it simpler not to alter the shape of their heads at all, or the style of their hair, and after some careful consideration simply "go with the Flo."

Thus, to have *all* the necessary background for determining which nursing school to attend, we say sincerely: "If the cap fits —and looks good—wear it!"

On and Off the Course
A Look at the Kind and Killer Courses

The usual nursing diploma program is three years. Entrance requires a high school diploma, good grades, and a white wardrobe. School costs range from $500 (Joe's Bargain Basement Hospital, Nursing School, and Used Car Showroom) to $5,000 per year (Tiffany's Hospital, Nursing School, and Diamond-Cutting Facility).

Here is a typical curriculum from a private hospital-affiliated school located somewhere in the Midwest.

First Year

HUMAN PHYSIOLOGY:	Study of biology, with emphasis on blood, gore, glop, and drippy things. DO NOT SCHEDULE AROUND LUNCHTIME!
INTRO TO PSYCHOLOGY:	Capsule summary of man's cognitive evolution from prehistoric apelike creatures to modern neurotics. Emphasis on Freud, Jung, Adler, Piaget, Westheimer, and Ann Landers.
INTRO. TO GENERAL CHEMISTRY:	Emphasis on atomic and molecular structures, such as hospital food and your roommate's cooking.
PHYSICAL EDUCATION:	GYM CLASS, AND THIS TIME YOU'RE NOT EXCUSED!
HUMAN PHYSIOLOGY 2:	The hipbone's connected to the leg bone, the leg bone's connected to the knee bone . . . without musical accompaniment.
BIOCHEMISTRY:	Two dreaded subjects in one! Emphasis on compound chemicals, and compound headaches.

First Year (Continued)

INTRO. TO SOCIOLOGY:
Study of society with emphasis on such popular American customs as reading sensationalistic magazines on line at the supermarket with no intention of buying them; why some Americans wipe the excess ketchup off the mouth of the bottle before putting the top back on; why Americans mail a letter, then double-check to see that it went down in the box; why we simonize, etc.

CHILD AND ADOLESCENT DEVELOPMENT:
How society, culture, heredity, Mr. Rogers, Big Macs, Mr. T, Madonna, masturbation, Rainbow Brite, *Friday The Thirteenth,* and Cherry Ames turn innocent children into "Adolescents."

PHYSICAL EDUCATION:
Rope-climbing. Essential and practical training for everyday nursing emergencies in high-rise health facilities without elevators, stairways, or fire escapes.

HUMAN PHYSIOLOGY 3:
From digesting to indigestion and back again.

HUMAN NUTRITION:
The seven basic food groups, which are now considered to be the four basic food groups, except in nine midwestern states who have six basic food groups, and Alaska and Hawaii who don't believe in basic food groups. You'll also study hospital food, which doesn't have a group. Prerequisite: Human Physiology 3.

NURSING CARE OF ADULTS AND THE ELDERLY, PART 1:
At last, the course that all the advice-seeking relatives and friends of the family are waiting for you take.

First Year (Continued)

MIDDLE AGE AND AGING:	A preview of your own personal metamorphosis in years two and three of this program.

Second Year

INTRO. TO NURSING SKILLS:	After one year and lots of money spent, you get to play nurse for the first time. Emphasis on dressings . . . Italian, French, Russian, Garlic.*
INTRO. TO PHARMACOLOGY:	Everything you ever wanted to know about the drugs you were afraid to try. Prominent people in drug history are studied: Salk, Leary, Cheech and Chong, The Grateful Dead, von Bulow. How to say no to personal requests from family and friends.
MICROBIOLOGY:	The dissection of previously dissected items into even smaller pieces.
PHYSICAL EDUCATION:	Body-building, with emphasis on lifting basically inanimate objects three times your weight.
O.R. NURSING INTRO.:	Guaranteed to start your diet by stopping your appetite.
COMMUNICATION WITH PHYSICIANS:	Alternate title: "Communication with the Dead." The methods—and the results—are the same.

* Editor: An accidental excerpt from the author's *Culinary Handbook*. Sorry.

Second Year (Continued)

NURSING CARE OF ADULTS, PART 2:	How to avoid family gatherings and visits by numerous family friends. Ways to fake amnesia for hypochondriac acquaintances. Methods of pretending you no longer speak English and therefore can't give free medical advice every time they see you.
ABNORMAL PSYCHOLOGY:	How to deal with interns and new residents.
MARRIAGE AND THE FAMILY:	Study of the basic family structure. How to find a husband and start a family in your limited spare time. Study of child patients and why mothers overrule all hospital authority.
MATERNITY NURSING:	Study of storks and cabbage patches.
HUMAN SEXUAL PROBLEMS:	Study of men at singles' bars, with emphasis on your last boyfriend.

Third Year

NURSING OF CHILDREN:	Fun and games, plus 101 ways of dealing with screaming brats.
CHARM AND BEDSIDE MANNER:	If the patient says the little blue pills are purple, then they're purple, just so long as he takes them. Learning, how to take abuse all day and dish it out to your loved ones at night. Learning the true definition of one stiff drink.

Third Year (Continued)

NURSING CARE OF ADULTS, PART 3:	How to approach and convince family, friends, and relatives that you haven't learned anything beneficial to them in a year and a half of schooling. In fact, you're toying with the idea of becoming a nun after all.
ADVANCED MICROBIOLOGY:	The further dissection of tissue dissected from previously dissected matter which had been dissected once before. Learning to work with extremely powerful microscopes. DO NOT SCHEDULE ON A MONDAY MORNING!
MANAGEMENT IN NURSING:	Leadership and how to keep your head while causing others to lose theirs. How to be a double agent, to be in charge, to delegate responsibility, and juggle twenty-two headaches at once, six of whom want to hang you, nine of whom want to shoot you, and eight of whom give you dirty looks.
MICROCULTURES:	Study of tiny forms of life such as pygmies, dwarfs, and munchkins.
HEADACHES 101:	How to treat your own—without Extra-Strength Tylenol™. Learning to deal effectively with doctors, residents, interns, orderlies, aides, visitors, and others who may interfere with the performance of your nursing duties.

A Shot in the Dark

Learning to Give Injections

If you don't like receiving injections, giving them may also take a bit of getting used to. Fortunately for the rest of society, you won't get the opportunity until you have had a bit of practice on inanimate objects. Since neither plywood, sheetmetal, nor toaster ovens prove easy to puncture, fruit is a common victim for these first inoculations. But many nursing students question the validity of giving shots without having worthwhile ammunition. To combat this dilemma, there developed the popular trend of injecting oranges with a bit of vodka. This practice provides a further purpose to your inoculations, resulting in "juiced-up" fruit, a superb after-class treat.

Nonetheless, there reaches a point where you will graduate to working in a real hospital (or the local produce market, depending on how well you've done thus far). A real hospital presents a new twist to injections—real people, with veins instead of pulp. The key to your first injection is to remain calm, don't ramble, don't fidget, try not to be thirsty, and most important, don't let on that this is the first injection you've ever given. If you look young and inexperienced, you may prompt a patient to inquire how many injections you've already administered. Bearing your fruitful experience in mind, your answer should be, "Oh, bushels of them!"

The Student Nurse's Nemesis: Instructors
A Brief Guide

THEORETICAL THELMA

"It's not important that he's not eating—what's important is *why*." Thelma's main concerns are the reasons *behind* what is going on. "It's not how you play the game, it's *why* you play it in the first place." This knowledge will create a better, richer appreciation of your job. On the other hand, scrutinizing the "hows" and "whys" of emptying bedpans and giving enemas often leads to "don'ts," "won'ts," and a jaundiced view of human functions.

METICULOUS MARY

"We'll stop the bleeding later—just make sure those corners are tucked in and that he has three towels, not two or four!" Mary is the one who left the WACs to make sure hospital rooms are neat enough to meet military specifications. Her belief is that a meticulous room is a healthy room, even if the patient doesn't live to see it.

NEOPHYTE NORA

"I think it's done that way, but let me just check." Nora isn't much further down the nursing road than you are, and her confidence level in what she's teaching begins in the basement. She's hopeful you'll do things so well that she'll learn something too. "Oh, you're right. It *is* done that way," she may exclaim gleefully. But as much as you may crave a kind word, don't make the mistake of believing her!

ACTIVIST ANNA

"Policies can always be changed! You can't let the system dictate your lives! All together say 'Norma Rae!' Louder!" A modern Florence Nightingale out to change the world, Anna is not satisfied with the way things are. "She Is Woman, She Is Nurse." At 1960s rallies, Anna treated burns from bra and draft card burnings. Filled with fervor, she is determined to see you stand up for yourselves. In fact, she might have you on strike for better working conditions—before you've even seen working conditions in the hospital.

INVISIBLE INEZ

"That's not the proper method for changing a dressing!" These words are important in learning correct procedures, but what about when you start hearing them in your spare hours at home? Inez is that one instructor who somehow manages to be everywhere—she's omnipresent. She's George Orwell's Big Brother (or in this case, Big (Nurse). It's uncanny how she knows you've folded the sheets wrong on the third floor, while she's having lunch on the first. In time you'll be convinced that she's simply invisible. She sees you when you're sleeping and knows when you're awake . . .

Some nursing instructors will take you under their wings and guide you, while others will take you under their beaks and peck at you. A talented future nurse learns to ask good questions, smile, have good strong reasons (or good excuses) for everything she does. And, as they say on television, never let them see you sweat.

Tricks of the Trade: Learning to Be Cheerful —No Matter What

How does one maintain a pleasant demeanor throughout all sorts of chaos, turmoil, and grief? There are ways of training yourself to build a stiff upper (and lower) "smiling" lip. Here is a list of twenty-five items. Could you keep on smiling through them? Well, maybe not now, but once you become a nurse, they'll seem like child's play!

Can you smile through:

1. Twenty-five hours of *Father Knows Best, Make Room for Daddy,* or *Lifestyles of the Rich and Famous?*
2. Having your umbrella turn inside out seventeen times in a torrential rainstorm—and losing your shoe in a puddle so deep that it was declared a lake?
3. Two hours of listening to your fiancé(e)'s parents talk lovingly about his (her) "previous" girlfriend (boyfriend)?
4. A Three Stooges film festival?
5. The final scene in the late seventies remake of *The Champ?* Any part of *E.T.* or *Love Story?*
6. A week-long visit from your folks?
6 a. With your in-laws?

7. The sixth month of your boyfriend's impotence?

8. Three hours of your neighbor's six-year-old playing drums?

9. A three-week-long garbage strike?

9 a. In August?

10. A presidential speech, the news team's entire analysis, followed by *The Eleven O'-Clock News?*

11. An argument with your landlord over no hot water for one full week?

11 a. In January?

12. Having fifteen relatives cancel on you after you've made your first Thanksgiving turkey?

13. An entire Twisted Sister album?

13 a. With videos?

14. A double date where your boyfriend keeps looking at the other girl?

14 a. Other boy?

15. Staying in your teaching hospital as a patient—In traction?

16. A blind date with a guy whose favorite movie is *The Sensuous Nurse* (and he can quote from it)?

17. Buying meat at today's prices, waiting on line to pay for it, and finding out once you've gotten home that the steak you bought was buffalo meat?

18. The aftereffects of your two-year-old niece trying to flush an apple down the toilet?

19. Finding your spouse in bed with a candy striper?

20. An hour of listening to Norman Mailer speak?

20 a. Reading his latest book?

21. Seeing your new boyfriend's photo in the post office on the FBI's Most Wanted list?

22. Two hours of delousing your son's hair . . . followed by your daughter's . . . followed by your own?

23. Your first visit to the dentist in two years?

24. A return visit to the dentist the following week, and ten of them thereafter?

25. Your neighbors accidentally parking their station wagon on your front lawn?

25 a. In your den?

Your Smile Quotient

If you made it through the whole list, you're (choose one): (A) Mother Theresa (B) on drugs, or (C) living in another dimension.

If you made it halfway through this list and kept on smiling, you're indeed a born nurse and/or masochist.

If you couldn't make it even halfway through, don't feel bad. The world is a tough place. Ask a nurse—but don't be one.

ON THE CHARTS
Abbreviations for R.N.'s

Communication is so important between nurses who rotate rounds. When a nurse picks up a patient's chart, she must immediately pick up information vital to the patient's care—information forbidden to said patient and his or her family. For this reason, nurses have established a system of abbreviations known only to them. Here are some of the most common ones used:

aa	of each
abb	abbreviation
a.m.	after meals
A.C.	another chance
A.C.P.	another chance, please?
ba	bath or sheep
bh	bitch
b.i.d.	twice a day
b.i.t.	patient bit me
c.	with
ca.ca.	feces
caps.	capsules
cups.	cups
cu.p	cute patient
DD	Dunkin' Doughnuts/Dolly Parton
D.W.	distilled water
Dty. W.	dirty water
E.L.P.	eats like pig
fl./fld.	fluid/flood
F.P.N.	forgot patient's name
fsb.	fussbudget
fx	good action film
fu!	darn!
G.G.	I've got some Great Gossip
gm.	gram
gtt.	drop
gttd.	dropped
gttdb.	dropped and broke
H.J.?	Howard Johnson's after work?
H.N.O.W.	head nurse on warpath
H.S.	hour of sleep

H.X.S.	haven't had an hour of sleep all week
I.R.S.	trouble
IV	intravenous
IVD	intravenous de Milo
Kg.	kilogram
KGB	Russian spy
KHN	killaheadnurse
KKK	wears sheets
L.F.	left fielder
liq.	liquid
liq. B.O.	stinks from alcohol
mcg.	microgram
mcg., B.	Billigram
oz.	ounce
Oz	where Dorothy, Toto, and the Tin Man went
pacm.	Pacman
per os.	by mouth
per oe.	by ear
pin	pain in the neck
pp	urine specimen
pte.O.	paté only!
QDr.	quack doctor
q.h.	every hour
q.2h	every two hours
q.9Y	every nine years
q.H.C.P.	every time Halley's Comet passes
R.U.K.	are you kidding?
Rx	take
Rx!	take it or else!
Rx2Cam.	take two and call me in the morning
sig.	write on label
sin.	write on nose
six	6
S.S.	soapsuds/Soupy Sales
sol.	solution
Sol. R.	Sol Rabinowitz
Sp.	spelling error
sumo	patient knows wrestling
tbsp.	tablespoon
tsp.	teaspoon

tgsp.	Teri Garr's spoon
TV	transvestite
TV SET	obstinate transvestite
vt.	I'm very tired
ung.	ointment
unm.	oatmeal
W.B.	we're Beatrice
W.H.	well hung
X	sign here
X$	sign here, then pay
zzz	sleeping

Sometimes nurses abbreviate entire sentences, assuming you'll understand what they mean. For instance, the abbreviation O.O.B.S.H.W.C.ba# is translated as follows: *Patient was out of bed wandering the halls and got run over during a wheelchair race but is doing fine now back in his room resting comfortably after having eaten and bathed.*

CHAPTER THREE

This R.N. for Hire

Hospitality
or
Finding Your Niche Can Be a Bitch

Following the pomp of graduation, the circumstance of searching for a nursing job can be somewhat of a letdown. Once the celebration party hangover subsides, you may have to ask yourself a few down-to-earth questions, such as: Where do I choose to live? What are my career goals? What are my personal goals? Where's the vodka?

There are many doors open to nurses, and you may therefore wish to peer into a few of them:

Staying Put

Say you have just finished training at a specific hospital. In this situation, you may choose to apply for a job at that very institution. Although this limits your job hunt to a safari in your own backyard, you may enjoy the cozy feeling you get from fa-

miliar surroundings. On the other hand, familiarity sometimes breeds contempt, especially on your new 2:00 A.M. shift. (You also should consider the fact that you may already have run through all the interns, residents, and M.D.'s on the staff who are even vaguely "eligible.")

On the Road

You may leave the local life for a bit of traveling. Nurses are in greater demand in many other parts of the country—and the world. You might find yourself deciding between neighborhoods: Do I take the job by the nuclear power plant, or the one in the area with the highest crime rate in the continental United States? You could even be deciding between countries: Is Mandarin Chinese easier to learn than Arabic?

The Call of the Wild

When it comes to traveling, quite often you need not hunt down the job—it will hunt you down. Hospital recruiters rival insurance salesmen as they attempt to lure you to their exotic locales with sales pitches that rival Club Med. "Enjoy swimming, sailing, snorkeling, camping . . . that is, if your insane rotation shifts allow it." Some hospitals far afield offer such great benefits as an apartment, a new car, extra vacation time, immunity from all state and city laws, your own fast food franchise, and many others. A great many of these offers sound intriguing, but don't forget to ask salient questions, like: Do I get paid in actual currency as opposed to livestock? Does the hospital have indoor plumbing? Is there a bar within a hundred miles? Is the life expectancy there over thirty?

Agencies and Personnel Pools

These positions are great for the nurse on the go, because that's what you'll be doing—going from one hospital or clinic to another. These are services that send nurses to hospitals where they are needed—often desperately. Here you'll have the opportunity to get lost in every hospital in town, while checking out neighborhoods you had only seen previously on the eleven o'clock news. (On the other hand, the good news is that the coworker who rubbed you the wrong way yesterday probably won't have the opportunity for further rubbing tomorrow.)

Anti-Hospitality

Nursing is not confined to hospitals. You might lean toward the free-lance life as a private nurse to the handicapped, the elderly—or the eccentric billionaire. Also, doctors need nurses in their offices five days a week, even if the M.D.'s themselves are only there for two of them. In the warmer months, job ads appear for summer camp nurses. There are some advantages to these positions. Mosquito bites and poison ivy won't provide a major challenge, but you'll be able to get a tan—and all the adolescent crushes you can handle. Cruise ships can also provide a great tan, plus the opportunity to see the world while specializing in seasickness, sunburn pain, and the avid attentions of oversexed cabin boys.

Finding the right nursing job can be arduous, as is the case with finding any job. Interviews are as much fun as entrance exams, but they lead to your just desserts—salaried jobs. Some come with a creamy filling while others go stale quickly, but that's what being an R.N. (Real Nurse) in the R.W. (Real World) is all about. Happy hunting!

Want Ads: Reading Between the Lines

WHAT THE AD SAID:	WHAT IT REALLY MEANT:
Job requires ability to work pleasantly with the public in a busy pediatrician's offiice.	Can you give shots and take blood from moving objects; sing, dance, and entertain screaming brats; calm crazed patients; and keep on smiling twelve hours a day?
Wanted: school nurse able to relate meaningfully to the students.	We need someone with enough brains to tell the difference between cutting a finger and cutting a class.
Seeking recent graduate for newly established private practice. Will train.	"Hi! I'm a young, single doctor. I just thought I'd put in a personal, uh, *personnel* ad.
Nurse needed to work in geriatric facility. Interest in senior citizens essential.	We want someone who thinks of visits from grandparents as something other than a possible opportunity to inherit big money.
Good learning experience for R.N. sensitive to the needs of underprivileged children. Room for advancement.	The clinic is in a dangerous neighborhood and the pay is low. Why else do you think there's such a rapid turnover?
Outrageous 25K! Busy corp. seeking RN. Work as a team member. Great benefits, great location!	We're gonna offer you the world . . . at a price. You'll be up to your corporate neck in paperwork and then some . . . and since this is an agency ad, you'd better type fast!
Seeking innovative self-starter with fresh ideas and a supervisory background, for new facility.	We have no idea yet what this job entails, or what you'll be doing, so think of something and tell the rest of us.
Major company seeks p/t nurse for physical exams. Excellent benefits for right applicant.	If the physicals come out in the insurance company's favor, you're the right candidate . . . catch our drift, sweetheart?

How to Survive a Job Interview

Job interviews are specifically designed for three basic purposes:

1. To find out (generally) about your skills and (specifically) how easily you perspire.
2. To see how well you can endure humiliating, belittling, dehumanizing situations.
3. To bolster up the sadistic ego of the interviewer.

Important Things to Remember During Interviews

1. *Make eye contact.* Don't stare, but don't look down a lot—it makes the interviewer think that either you are insecure, dozing off, or that he or she has something on his/her shoe.
2. *Be a good listener.* Don't sing or whistle when the interviewer is talking, and don't wear a Walkman, a stethoscope, earmuffs, or earplugs.
3. *Be agreeable.* Nod a lot—but don't overdo it. You don't want to look like the little furry animals people keep on their dashboards. If you must disagree, do it tactfully. Avoid saying things like, "That's the stupidest thing I've ever heard" or "It's just that kind of sick, perverted attitude that's ruining America today" or "You belong in the mental ward—do you know that?"
4. *Be confident in your answers and ask pertinent questions.* Speak loudly enough so that the interviewer can hear you, but not the entire first floor. Try to avoid pounding your fist on the desk for emphasis. Ask questions about the hospital and the immediate job, but avoid dwelling on whether you will receive a promotion in three or four days. Don't ask about the pictures of the spouse and lovely children on the interviewer's desk—for all you know, they're in the middle of a heated custody battle. (They may, in fact, not be a family at all, but those paper photos that come with the frame when purchased.)

What to Say During a Job Interview:
Sample Q's and A's

Following are some sample interview questions nurses may be asked. We hereby provide some "good" answers (along with some other answers that may just cross your mind).

Q. *Why would you like to work here?*
A. Because I've heard that this hospital has an excellent reputation for patient care.

Because I didn't get accepted by the ten other hospitals I applied to, and this is the only place left that's in a relatively decent neighborhood.

Because I was once a patient in this horrible place, and I want to make others suffer the way I did.

Q. *What do you consider your strong points?*
A. I'm adaptable to new and challenging situations, work well with others, and consider myself well organized.

Being able to put up with your idiotic questions and condescending attitude while still maintaining a charming smile.

I think my strongest point is being able to shriek at people in decibels that only dogs can hear and that will also mysteriously shatter all the glass in the hospital!

Strong points? I'm smarter than anyone you have on your entire staff!

Q. *What do you feel you can give of yourself to this hospital?*
A. My caring attitude, compassion for patients, and ability to work as a team member.

What do you want, a signed organ donor card? How about a pint of blood on my way out?

I make a great meatloaf and mean martinis!

Q. *What do you want from this position?*
A. I'd like the opportunity to display my skills and use my fresh ideas to help the staff and patients.

I'd like more money, a car—a new coat would be nice . . . maybe a paid trip to the Bahamas, jewelry, some municipal bonds, an acre of prime real estate in California . . .

Q. *Right now, what is the most important thing in your life?*
A. Having a successful nursing career and starting on the road to financial security.

Getting through this interview without throwing up all over your desk.

Finding a job so I can get out of debt and not be a disgrace to my family after all that schooling.

Become queen of a small oil-producing nation.

Watching *Dynasty* on TV.

Q. *How do you deal with conflicts on the job?*
A. I discuss the matter with my supervisor and the other people involved, gather all the information, and then work toward the most practical, effective solution.

Could you be more specific? How in the hell do I know if you don't tell me what kind of conflicts?

I try to sweep things under the rug if possible. If that fails, I blame others for what goes wrong.

Generally, I bitch a lot.

Q. *Would you mind if I call your former employer for a reference?*
A. No, not at all. I'm sure she'll give me a strong and fair recommendation.

That bitch! She'll probably tell you about the time I forgot the bathrooms were being painted and gave all the patients enemas.

Q. *Do you have any office experience?*
A. Yes, I was assistant to the President for six years.

No, I just got tired of being part of the family's high-wire circus act and thought I'd just wander in here off the street.

Q. *Do you feel that you can handle the responsibilities of a busy doctor's office?*
A. I feel very comfortable in a busy environment.

It depends on how obnoxious your patients are . . . and I'm not touching that fish tank!

No, but I'll try to pull it off until you catch on.

Doctor's office? From the sound of your patients, you should hire a plumber—or a policeman.

HOW TO ACT ON AN INTERVIEW:
A Quickie Quiz

1. The proper attire for a job interview is:

   (A) An all-white evening gown, complete with all-white accessories
   (B) A tailored business suit.
   (C) A rental nurse's uniform.

2. If the interviewer asks a question you are not prepared to answer, you should:

   (A) Become defensive and hostile.
   (B) Phone someone long distance and get the correct answer.
   (C) Get up and storm out of the office.

3. If the interviewer asks you about politics, religion, or any subject you consider personal, you should:

   (A) Politely avoid answering the question.
   (B) Throw a small desk lamp at the interviewer's head.
   (C) Give the interviewer your personal diary.

4. During an interview you should:

   (A) Sit up.
   (B) Spit up.
   (C) Stand up.
   (D) Drink 7UP.
   (E) All of the above.

5. If asked to describe your nursing skills, you should:

   (A) Give a brief description of what you do best.
   (B) Give the interviewer a bath, injection, and sleeping pill.
   (C) Explain that you don't have any skills but hope to learn some on the job.

6. To an interview, you should bring:

   (A) Your résumé, since s/he will have misplaced the one you sent.
   (B) A sandwich and a soda, in case s/he keeps you waiting.
   (C) Friends to back up whatever you say in three-part harmony.
   (D) A tape recorder so that anything the interviewer says can and will be held against her or him.

7. You should never ask an interviewer:

   (A) If s/he just passed gas.
   (B) How much money s/he'd accept as a bribe to give you the job.
   (C) If that's his or her real hair.
   (D) Any of the above.

8. At an interview you should be seated:

   (A) Across from the interviewer.
   (B) In the yoga lotus position.
   (C) On the desk dangling your feet out the window.

9. If the interviewer hires you on the spot, you should:

   (A) Thank him or her politely, smile, and ask when you should start.
   (B) Assume that something fishy is going on and demand an explanation—and a raise.
   (C) Break open a bottle of champagne and a jar of beluga caviar.
   (D) Jump up and down, kiss and hug the interviewer, and run through the halls screaming out your joy.

10. If the interviewer hires you on a trial basis, this means:

   (A) They want to see how you work before committing themselves.

(B) They're going to make you pay them for the opportunity to work in the hospital.

(C) They want you to work in a courtroom.

(D) Someone will probably stand over you at all times quoting the nursing manual, Florence Nightingale's biography, and scenes from the film *Carry on Nurse*.

Answers

There are no easy answers. Interviews are really a matter of personal style, after all.

Buying a Stethoscope

Stethoscopes range in price from $20 to $300. You should choose one priced somewhere in between since you'll want to show that you're serious about your work without being ostentatious. Look for something with two heads that's light, comfortable, and in "your" color. Pretend you're headphone shopping. Once you've chosen one, try it out at home. Start with family and friends. Then, when they're tired of playing patient, try household appliances. Can you hear inner workings of the TV? How does the dishwasher sound? Everthing okay in the rinse cycle? Can you hear the clock ticking? How about your brother's digital watch?

Helpful hint: When buying a stethoscope, act intelligent. Don't ask where the volume knob is, or about the bass and treble balance.

Types of Nurses: A Field Guide

As with flowers, nurses come in a variety of shapes, sizes, and colors. They come with all kinds of temperaments and personalities as well. In the hospital or other place of practice you have chosen, you will come to notice that the genus "nurse" divides itself into certain recognizable categories or species. Following are some of the stereotypical nurses you will encounter on your appointed rounds. Study them; get to know all their strengths and weaknesses. See if you can recognize the future you.

SWEET SUZIE, INNOCENT IDA, OR VIRGINAL VIRGINIA

The most angelic of the nursing species, these perpetually sweet R.N.'s retain the dewy-eyed wonder of a sophomore at her first prom. Their soulful gaze is that which most others reserve for newborn puppies. Male patients respond by rolling over and wagging their tails—and falling madly in love with these often-ineffectual angels of mercy. Sweet Suzie is far from efficient, spending most of her time fetching vases or fruit juice —but patients feel compelled to get better simply to avoid breaking this poor nurse's heart.

(However, said patients had better pray she's not on duty if they go into cardiac arrest.)

BATTLE-AX BERTHA

Reminiscent of the nurse in *One Flew Over the Cuckoo's Nest*, these R.N.'s mean business! Lights out means lights out—it doesn't matter if another nurse is taking blood at the time. These tough mamas didn't make it into the Marines, so they're revolting (are they ever!). Don't even think of crossing them, because they've got the rules on their side (often tattooed on their bulging biceps). Bertha can't for the life of her understand how anyone pulling a double shift could feel overworked. Need it be said that her favorite patients are Hell's Angels, pro wrestlers, and hit men? She dreams about serving hospital food to Rambo—and forcing him to eat it. Battle-ax Berthas are certain half of the patients shouldn't be "lazing around" in the hospital to begin with, and the positive function of these distaff dictators is intimidating patients into feeling healthy enough to check out.

LAZY LUCY

Call light on? She "didn't see it." She's not tired from long shifts and being overworked: she's tired from staying up all night thinking up excuses for goofing off. She'll "get around to it eventually," but starting her morning rounds at 11:55 is pushing it a bit. Lucy is completely aware of what has to be done, and equally sure that if she doesn't do it, someone else will . . . she hopes. True, Lazy Lucy is therapeutically beneficial to many patients, who learn to do for themselves out of desperation. She can usually be found using the phone for an "emergency at home," or engaging in her favorite hospital activities—chatting and gossiping. Steer clear of this one, or you'll find yourself making her rounds—while she sneaks off to the nurses' lounge to watch *General Hospital*.

MOTHER MOLLY

Molly is a bit older, and therefore a bit wiser than the average nurse. Loaded to the gills with anecdotes of her nursing past, she's sincere, steadfast, and thorough—possibly *too* thorough. With five blankets, three of them thermal, a heating pad, a woolen bathrobe, and a sleeping pill that began working fifteen minutes ago, it's reasonable to conclude that waking a patient to find out if he or she is too cold might be unnecessary. Molly just wants to make sure that patients eat and sleep well. She wants to be sure the residents, nurses, orderlies, elevator operators, and visitors eat

and sleep well. If you're single, she'll matchmake. If you're tired, she'll find you a place to rest. If you're hungry, she'll bring you home-baked cookies. She reads *Good Housekeeping* and *Readers' Digest,* talks about her family and their ailments, crochets—and wakes patients up to take their sleeping pills.

SEXY SADIE

White fishnet stockings, miniskirted uniforms, and gallons of perfume are her trademarks. Because she goes braless, Sadie must *by all means* be kept away from the cardiac unit. She's *The Sensuous Nurse* in the flesh. In school, her only high grades were in biology, and even then she need "special tutoring sessions" from the prof. Sadie gets consistently high temperature readings from her male patients, and they often develop high blood pressure—as do the doctors. She always knows where there's an empty bed—and she makes sure it doesn't stay empty for long. She loves to work the night shift and will often yell "STAT" when there's a cute resident on duty. Sexy Sadie's greatest nursing skills are bringing male patients out of comas, keeping elderly men in absolutely top form, with their reflexes sharp, and motivating female patients to get well quickly so their male visitors won't be tempted by Sadie again.

BITCHIN' BRENDA

No matter how overworked and exhausted you are, Brenda is more so. This little princess got everything she wanted, and she really thought nursing would be a breeze. Her diligence is far surpassed by her complaining—in fact, she bitches and moans enough for the entire shift, making her a true wonder in the morale department. If Brenda won the lottery, the first thing she'd do would be bitch about not finding a bank close by enough to deposit the money at. In Brenda's life, nothing is *ever* right. Her boyfriend's new Renault doesn't have enough leg room, and besides, it rained the whole first day of their Caribbean vacation. Brenda chose the wrong profession—and she is vociferous about this fact. She finds it depressing to be around sick people, and will often complain to ICU patients (those who are conscious, that is) about her ruined manicure. Her greatest asset to the patients is that after listening to her gripe and bitch, they not only don't feel so bad, but they start gathering the strength either to kill her or go home.

TATTLETALE TINA

Tina is extremely observant: no detail of hospital life, no matter how petty, escapes her eagle eye and sharp tongue. She's often the head nurse's pet, since she keeps the head nurse informed about potential blackmail situations and malpractice suits—as well as humane rule-bending on the part of her fellow staff members. Her eye for details, such as cigarette butt brands, lipstick stains, and alcohol on the breath, would qualify her for a career as a private detective or medical examiner, but she prefers to be a petty, back-stabbing hospital snoop. Tattletale Tina might even make an excellent nurse, if only she would turn her eagle-eyed attentions to the patients under her care.

What's a Weekend?

How to Survive Nursing Shifts and Rotation

Nursing is not one of those nine-to-five jobs Dolly Parton complained about in her famous song. In fact, anyone who has experienced the typical nurse's schedule might well develop a new appreciation for "Workin' Nine to Five." For a nurse, the hours may be more like three to eleven, seven to four, ten to eight, or any other bizarre combination of the above. Nor can nurses relate to the joyful expression "Thank God it's Friday," since all too often their work week doesn't even contain a weekend.

The typical nurse's schedule will require some major rethinking and adaptation on your part, since you'll often find yourself unwinding from your workday while others are in dreamland, on their way to work, or out to lunch. Initially you may find yourself calling friends and family to chat, oblivious to the fact that the wall clock reads 5:00 A.M. It's disheartening, wanting to discuss the rigors of *your* day when theirs hasn't even begun. And it's disorienting to awaken just in time for the six o'clock news—at 6:00 P.M.! But believe it or not, in time you'll adjust. Soon you'll come to think of having Johnny Carson as your breakfast companion, going out on Monday night dates, and opening your Christmas gifts a few days later, as normal.

In fact, there are some actual advantages to the crazed schedule the hospital has stuck you with. You may not have noticed them at first, mainly because you were always asleep. Here are some of them.

The Advantages of Working Nights, Sleeping Days, and Never Having Two Days Off in a Row:

1. With your schedule, if someone wants to date you, rest assured that he really likes you. It's not every guy who'd call in sick in order to spend three hours on a Thursday morning with you.
2. You'll save money that you might otherwise have spent on weekend outings, holiday gifts, or social affairs that you're unable to attend.

3. You'll be able to avoid rush-hour hassles and traffic jams —and be able to find great parking spaces heretofore enjoyed only by the handicapped.
4. You'll be able to meet your mailman and garbageman personally, be first on line at your cash-card machine, and shape up with early-morning aerobics on TV.
5. You'll be able to use your work schedule as an excuse to get out of almost anything!
6. In case your schedule ever permits a long-distance vacation, jet lag will seem completely normal.

The Down Side

The worst part about rotation is that you're never really sure of your future and, therefore, end up rearranging your life so often that your social calendar resembles a Rorschach ink blot.

"No, Mom, but I can see you either this Thursday or next Tuesday . . . No, I have a date with Ronnie on Monday—or is that the following week? . . . Yes, I'd love to see Aunt Sally, but it'll have to be in two weeks . . . I don't know which day . . . I can't—I traded that Friday for a day off on Sunday to go to the wedding. . . . What do you mean, they postponed the wedding? They can't do this to me . . . I can't get another Sunday off until September, unless I trade Monday, but then I'll have to cancel dinner with Ronnie, and I haven't seen him in three weeks. . . . Yes, Mom, I'm eating just fine . . . For dinner? I don't really name my meals anymore, I just try to have two or three of them. . . . Have a good day, and . . . good night.''

One of the favorite pastimes brought about by rotating schedules is trading. Since Friday nights, Saturdays, and Sundays are prime time, they're worth much more than an insignificant Monday or Tuesday night. But the Boardwalk and Park Place of rotation are holidays. Thus, if you can parlay a Friday night, a Saturday, and a president's birthday for Thanksgiving and Christmas, you should really leave nursing and go into real estate or the stockmarket. Trading time off is a highly sophisticated skill combining a gambling instinct, manipulative powers, acting talent, and a knowledge of psychology. If your prowess in any of these areas falls short, you'd better check your loved ones into the hospital if you want to spend Thanksgiving and Christmas with them!

CHAPTER FOUR

Specialties of the Hospital

Nursing Supervisor

Ever wanted to rule a foreign country? Think of it: a place where no one will understand a thing you tell them to do—much less question it? Ever wonder how Gulliver felt in Lilliput or King Kong on the Empire State Building? As a nurse supervisor, you'll get to find out.

Your job is simply to know everything, go everywhere, and be everywhere, while remaining cool, calm, and collected. The nursing supervisor must be able to locate anything that's missing, including patients' personal belongings, new nurses, disappearing doctors, lost linen, forgotten files, misplaced medicine, and even an appropriated ambulance. Say a new wing is being added. The nursing supervisor had better know her way around before the foundation is finished.

But the supervisor's most important function is communica-tion—with everybody, often at the same time. Discussing the patient in 223 with a nurse, while a physician explains what must be done for the lady in 522, as you're directing a visitor to 417, while reading the chart from 323, and sending maintenance to 168, is simply routine.

Everything's your responsi-bility—hospital disasters, natural disasters, the health of everyone within a four-mile radius, and the fact that the hospital has only five floors. In short, if you should call in sick, you can bet that the building won't be standing when you return!

THE N.S. TEST
(Only *She* Gets a Test)

**Here's a little test to see if you have "the right stuff"
to become a nursing supervisor.**

Agree or Disagree?

1. When giving instructions, you should be as subtle as possible, using such phrases as "Give the patient in 318—or is it 19—some kind of medicine."

2. In the case of an emergency, by all means leave the building first, and assume the others will follow.

3. If someone asks the same question more than once, make sure to belittle them in front of the entire staff, using the P.A. system.

4. You should continuously remind the staff that the reason you're in charge is that you're more competent then any of them and can do anything in half as much time. Make sure you carry a stopwatch at all times to prove it.

5. It's a good idea to create and spread idle gossip about the nurses, patients, and doctors. Publish a *Hospital Enquirer* if possible. Talk to patients about other patients' personal problems. Ask their advice.

6. It never hurts to carry a bullwhip, wear black leather boots, or refer to the Marquis de Sade frequently.

7. Tell annoying patients what you really think of them as they're leaving, using facial expressions and hand gestures lavishly.

8. When unforeseen problems arise, insist that no matter what anyone else suggests, you're right and they're wrong. Stamp your feet and threaten them with bodily harm if necessary.

9. Quote from *Gone With The Wind* frequently: "Frankly, [Scarlett] I don't give a damn!"

10. By all means make sure that everyone realizes that deep down beneath your tough exterior, you really hate their guts.

11. Be as loud as possible. Good leadership means being heard—even by the deaf.

12. Go by the book! Do everything it says to the letter. It doesn't matter what book, as long as you stick to it. Memorize and spout as often as possible the invaluable bureaucratic phrase: "If we let you do that, then we'd have to let everyone do it."

13. Never, under any circumstances, even in the case of a heroic lifesaving act, compliment anybody.

14. Look over people's shoulders constantly; it'll do your staff good to have muscle spasms in their necks from turning to see if you're there.

15. Show obvious favoritism. It's good for morale to let patients and staff alike know that if so and so had done it you'd be pleased, because you like them better. Then smile and leave.

Test Results

Add up the number of statements you agreed with (if any) and check the results below:

0– 5   Your passive and human nature is totally unsuited to the position of nurse supervisor. In fact, you may lack the gumption even to be a nurse.

6–10   Nurse Rachett has nothing on you, sweetheart. You were born to supervise.

11–15 Your talents are too powerful for a mere hospital. Have you considered being a prison matron or mother superior?

The Emergency Room Nurse

Emergency room nursing is a peacetime equivalent to the M*A*S*H 4077th, with you as "Hot Lips" Houlihan trying to keep a cool head in the face of constant chaos. Unfortunately, there's no director to yell "Cut!" and end the scene. The emergency room is a twenty-four hour reality, and the props are genuine blood and guts.

Serious emergencies require a nurse to dip into her store of knowledge and training and react before the brain or digestive system have time to register a complaint. Emergency room nurses have little time to get to "know" their patients. The E.R. is the fast food equivalent to nursing, except that here you're dealing with "Mc-Humans."

Most nurses agree that the E.R. is a place in which you either love, or hate, to work. There's no in-between.

To survive in the E.R. means not questioning why a mother suddenly brings her daughter in at 3:00 A.M. complaining of a sore throat that has been equally sore for the past two weeks. It also means attempting triage in the face of patients' lack of co-operation. Drunks and vagrants pose the most difficult challenge when it comes to answering a few basic questions. However, a drunk singing opera and claiming to be Christopher Columbus can be a pleasure compared to the defiant patient who resents divulging any information about who he is and why he's graced you with his presence.

Another favorite among E.R. clientele is the mother/son team where junior *has* a pain, and the parent *is* one. "It hurts him in his stomach. It's his appendix—I know it. His father Arnie had his out in 1968—what a day that was. It almost burst right in the emergency room because we had to wait so long . . ." Meantime, Arnie, Jr., is not only capable of telling the nurse where it hurts, but also about the peanut butter and anchovy pizza he ate for lunch.

The E.R. nurse learns daily the meaning of the phrase, "expect the unexpected." No task is too awesome—or too ludicrous—for the emergency room to handle. Removing foreign objects from human bodies has become all too common these days. Contact delensing and hair delousing are nothing compared to the array of objects that sexual adventurers have been detached from in the E.R.! Trapped tampons and lost condoms are crassly commonplace; the proud E.R. can boast such items as a model spaceship found "launched" in a certain part of a young male patient's anatomy.

As in the case with so many popular nightspots, the E.R. attracts a large weekend crowd, especially in the summer months, when most athletes seeking the thrill of victory encounter instead the agony of defeat. Here, as she takes down the patient's history, the E.R.

nurse is treated to a play-by-play description of what happened.

Besides dealing with standing-room-only crowds in the summertime, the emergency room nurse has to keep a scorecard, line-up, and batting order at all times. Vying for position is a favorite pastime of E.R. patients. It's almost like a poker game—does a sprain beat dizziness?

One patient, insistent that he be next, will begin the bidding: "My cut is from a machete!"

The bid is soon raised. "Oh, yeah? Well, my leg was run over by a Sherman tank in the parking lot of K-Mart!"

"That's nothin'. This nuclear bomb, see, it exploded right outside my building!"

"Nurse, my son's appendix is going to burst just like his father's if you don't take us next!"

And so it goes. But it's the patient who demands to see the doctor immediately because his car is double-parked that truly tests the E.R. nurse's ability to remain polite. And it's the question, "Do you know who I am?" that tests her true mettle.

"No, sir, but please tell me so I can put your name on the waiting list."

That's the kind of reply E.R. nurses are famous for.

The Surgical Nurse

If germ warfare is your aim, then surgical nursing might be your game. Here's an opportunity to make up for all those times your mother had to remind you to wash up before dinner. In fact, you'll use more soap as a surgical nurse than some third-world nations see in a year.

Besides being cleaner than any mother's wildest dreams, as a surgical nurse you're in charge of seeing to it that the patient keeps his or her appointment with the knife. This can be difficult when patients wimp out at the last minute and simply refuse to go, clinging to the hospital corridors and shrieking. It's your job to reassure them that everything will be fine—even if you're lying through your teeth.

You may find *yourself* questioning the meaning of elective surgery. Does this mean a bunch of medics get together and vote on whether the patient should have surgery or not? No. Actually, surgery is even worse when it's dictated than when it's elected by the patient. In either case, it's important to remember that if local anaesthesia is being used, you should refrain from saying things like, "I can't believe he's going through with this," since a local doesn't impair the patient's hearing.

And don't forget that there's a lot of pre-op paperwork the patient is required to complete, clarifying which relative will inherit the doctor's watch should it end up inside said patient, and agreeing to the type of anaesthesia, be it a local, an express, or a shuttle to oblivion. This can pose quite a challenge. Getting a patient to sign forms while on the operating table is never easy; not only is it difficult for the patient to write while lying on his back, it's even harder if he's unconscious.

Studying M*A*S*H reruns closely will help you learn the surgical tools. It's important to know a scalpel from a scissors and a suture from a shoelace. For the first time in your life, those long-ago embroidery or knitting lessons from Grandma may come in handy.

One good thing about surgery is that the patient has no real opportunity to be exposed to the surgeon's personality. Unfortunately, you, the O.R. nurse, can't make the same claim. The O.R. nurse learns fast that surgeons are a strange breed. On the one hand, their minds are connected to their hands, and they can perform brilliant work for three, five, or eight hours. On the other, they then proceed to boast about their work for three, five, or eight days. As a rule tall and lanky, surgeons don't eat. (Let's face it, cutting into a rare steak or hunk of cherry pie must be a letdown after slicing into a live human organ in the life-or-death drama of the O.R.)

Surgeons don't laugh, either. In fact, they are largely devoid of human emotions, and they have little use for persons who are not under anaesthesia, often addressing them in one-syllable utterances. You will notice that these often begin with the letter s: "scalpel," "sutures," "syringe," "sponge," "stupid," etc.

Despite their sociopathic personalities, surgeons are often considered (especially by themselves) "stars," who perform in the "operating theater." Therefore, part of your job as an O.R. nurse is to play stage manager. You must be sure all the "props" (instruments) are ready, the lighting and temperature just right, and the "cast members" are in their proper costumes and positions.

If you close your eyes frequently during films like *The Texas Chain Saw Murders*, then surgical nursing is definitely not for you. However, if you want to work in a sparkling environment, if you like the smell of antiseptic, and if you enjoyed watching your father carve up roast beef as a child, then you may be perfect for a supporting role in the daily drama of the O.R.

The Psychiatric Nurse

The world of psychiatric nursing will put you in constant touch with the term "delusions of grandeur," since most psychiatrists you'll work with will suffer from this syndrome. The main reason psychiatrists are so overly confident is simple. You see, while mere M.D.'s can write prescriptions for boring antibiotics and painkillers, psychiatrists get to mete out powerful, mind-bending drugs that will make their patients act *any way they (the psychiatrists) want them to*.

A main function of psychiatric nurses is talking—and listening —to the pyschiatrists' patients. This often entails lengthy discussions with such personalities as Julius Caesar, Napoleon and Joan of Arc on such fascinating topics as ancient Rome, famous battles and French-style barbecues. It is to be hoped that you will quickly learn to keep a straight face and to accept others' senses of reality, no matter how unreal and far-removed from your own they seem to be.

Your skills at dealing with disturbed people will be further honed by encounters with their visiting friends and families, who often seem to embody the adage: "The apple doesn't fall far from the tree." (Is it any wonder that the son claims to be the Prince of Wales when the father comes in wearing the crown?)

Given that much of your time will be spent on such tasks as convincing paranoid patients that they shouldn't take the 250-pound security guards personally, helping Anne Boleyn search for her head, and keeping schizophrenic patients from beating themselves up, the mundane duty of giving out medica-

tion may seem like a relief. A relief, that is, until you realize how paranoid your charges are about their pills. Psychiatric patients are famous for hiding tablets under their tongues, or in more exotic orifices, out of certainty that you're trying to poison them. But think about it. Even paranoids have reason to fear mind-bending psychogenic preparations, not to mention Extra-Strength Tylenol capsules . . .

Psychiatric patients include those who were brought in by relatives, those who signed themselves in, and those who dropped in from another planet. Some are free to come and go, while others, who aren't free to come or go, will do so anyway. The latter can often be found in the operating arena, enjoying the "splatter"show, or sneaking a cup of hospital coffee in the nurses' lounge. (This may indicate a more severe disorder than anyone suspected.) Sometimes roaming psyc. patients even create hospital jobs for themselves, such as elevator operator in a fully automatic elevator, or doorman for a revolving door (which usually only lasts until they either get dizzy or get out).

There are, of course, those times when a patient believes he or she can overpower you, and is correct in this assumption. These are the times you'll appreciate tranquilizers, karate classes, and 250-pound killer guards. Medications are your helping hand for keeping the psychiatric ward in check. Just because the patients refuse to take their Thorazine, is that any reason *you* shouldn't?

One hazard of the psychiatric ward is that it may predispose you to analyze everyone you know—and even people you don't know. You could become the person most likely to be avoided at parties and social gatherings. (However, in some cases, this could actually turn out to be a plus.)

On the other hand, if you reach the point where you're explaining to the bus driver that the reason he drives so slowly is due to insecurity caused by falling off a tricycle at the age of three, you know it's time to transfer to another unit, another bus—or both.

The Male Nurse

She's a he? That's the patient's and visitor's common reaction to finding out that the nurse's name is "Jerry" and not "Jerri."

Life isn't easy for the man in a field dominated (97 percent) by women. Popular assumptions about the male nurse are that he's either gay, a perverted voyeur, or too dumb to be a doctor. Generally none of these assumptions are true, but it does seem that society needs an explanation as to what a guy is doing in

white if he's not a doctor or selling Good Humor ice cream. It's not uncommon to hear a patient telling a female nurse: "This orderly came in here and gave me my shot. Can he do that?"

The male nurse must have a healthy ego and an excellent sense of humor in order to withstand the insulting remarks and weird reactions he elicits from every quarter. Flirtatious young female patients change their tune when they find out the man in the room is not an "eligible" doctor. His female coworkers assume that, though he's not the head nurse, he's going to act as if he were. Male doctors are in an awkward spot. It's slightly more difficult for a short, skinny M.D. to yell at a six-foot, 220-pound R.N. than at a more "petite" version. Female doctors are often overly harsh in exercising the authority they have over male nurses (even if some secretly fantasize about "getting down" with them).

The male nurse chooses his schools the same way the female nurse does—by the cap. However, in his case, the question is: In which school will I have the least trouble when I refuse to wear the cap?"

There are benefits to being a male nurse. For one thing, guilt is on your side. Once your coworkers accept you, they'll often show you extra kindness in an effort to overcompensate for treating you so badly before. Nonetheless, no matter how

PSYCHOLOGY QUIZ*

1. The father of psychology is:
- (A) Sigmund Freud
- (B) George Washington
- (C) Joe Psychology

2. Acrophobia is
- (A) Fear of open places
- (B) Fear of acrobats
- (C) Fear of agriculture

3. Pavlov's dogs:
- (A) Salivated at the sound of a bell.
- (B) Were the group that did the punk rock version of "Puppy Love."
- (C) Won the stupid-pet-tricks competition on the *David Letterman Show*.

4. In August:
- (A) All therapists are required by law to take a vacation.
- (B) All psychologists are required by law to take a vacation.
- (C) All psychiatrists are required by law to take a vacation.
- (D) All of the above.

5. An Oedipus complex is:
- (A) A Freudian term for a child's libidinal feelings for the parent of the opposite sex.
- (B) The Greek god of blindness, and his twin brother.
- (C) A housing development in Oedipus, Missouri.

6. A person who thinks he is of much greater status than he really is:
- (A) Has delusions of grandeur.
- (B) Is a government employee.
- (C) Is a resident.
- (D) Is a psychiatrist.

7. A person claiming to be Julius Caesar:
- (A) Would make a good husband and provider.
- (B) Can make one hell of a salad.
- (C) Probably *is* Julius Caesar.
- (D) Most likely none of the above.

---

* All right, so we said only the N.S. got a quiz. Well, we're doing this because . . . we *feel* like it.

well accepted you are at the hospital, a redneck bar still might not be the best place for you proudly to announce your profession.

Even the most successful male nurse has to deal with some ticklish problems related to choosing a career dominated by the opposite sex. Some of these are:

Where to change your clothes
Whereas the ladies have a locker room, you're still not allowed inside no matter how well you've been accepted. Thus, your options include:

• Using the custodial quarters;
• Slipping behind the curtain of a bed you hope will remain empty another five minutes;
• Playing Supernurse in a phone booth;
• Finding a broom closet unoccupied by illicit lovers.

How to take a shower when you really need one
Your best bet is to use the doctors' shower room. After all, naked you can easily pass for a doctor, especially if you push your stomach out and then pretend to be holding it in while shaking your hands dry. Wearing a surgical mask might also help.

How to prove you're not gay
First of all, the best way is *not* to grab at the tempting tops and bottoms of your female coworkers. Even though this might

offer proof positive to discerning females that you're hetero, they'd still hate you, especially the female doctors. Also, try to resist the temptation of bragging to interns, residents, and M.D.'s about your wild sexual exploits with women, as this could also engender jealousy and hatred. Ultimately, the best way to prove that you're a red-blooded heterosexual male nurse is by *not* doing certain things. Never, never, under any circumstances:

• Arrange flowers for your patients;
• Give them advice on makeup and hairstyles;
• Give a sponge bath to any ambulatory male patient, espe-

cially if he begs you to do so. If necessary, bribe candy stripers to perform these tasks for you.

How to cope with rude questions and comments

Male nurses constantly have to field innuendos and outright insults. Here's a list of trenchant retorts that will come in handy both on and off the job:

- "Florence is dead, so get off my case!"
- "No, Mom, I don't wear white stockings!"
- "No, I didn't flunk out of med school—I didn't even apply."
- "If you want me to lift your heavy patients, then you have to empty my heavy bedpans."
- "Just because I have them doesn't give you the right to bust them!"

The OB-GYN Nurse

Do you thrive on laborious tasks? Well, OB-GYN nursing will have you doubled over, and not from laughter. Watching and waiting for the big moment —big moment—big moment— and hoping they don't all happen at once is your responsibility with a wardful of women in labor. And if you've ever wanted to judge Olympic time trials, here's your golden opportunity to keep your finger on the stopwatch as you help time their contractions.

If you remember *I Love Lucy, The Odd Couple, The Dick Van Dyke Show,* and practically every other TV sitcom where a baby was born, then you'll know how not to act when the big moment arrives. But the term "piece of cake" is hard to swallow when you realize that you're stage manager for the big event. Yes, you've been elected to locate the doctor, calm the prospective father, reassure the mother-to- be—and assist a precious new life into the world if push comes to shove and the doctor is playing golf.

Accommodating the mother's wishes is important on this big day, no matter how innovative or bizarre her chosen method of delivery may be. Whether it's the Jacques Cousteau underwater maneuver, birth by aerobics, or a live rock video production, the end result is bringing a new life into the world—with your help.

Making faces is a prerequisite for OB-GYN nurses, who have the honor of being the first to entertain the newest of audiences in the nursery. Often you'll find yourself playing to screams and cries and loving it. (At least you know they won't get up and leave—especially the incubator cases.) Many hospitals have the additional prerequisite that the OB-GYN nurse have at least one child of her own. This can, however, be a detriment to maternity patients' repeat visits, once you start talking about the terrible twos, frantic fours, and treacherous teens. (It also may not be worth the trouble of finding a mate and having a child for the sole purpose of working in OB-GYN.)

Acquainting fathers and newborns can be as smooth as ushering a bull on a skateboard through a china shop. Once Dad catches on, though, he'll have to be pried away from the nursery window. Meanwhile, the postpartum unit is where you'll start teaching the new mother everything from feeding and bathing her baby to explaining the difference between a hungry cry, a cranky cry, and a husband's lack-of-attention cry.

OB-GYN nurses often develop a love for soft pinks and blues; frequently they are closet applesauce freaks who have meaningful relationships with stuffed toys. The only real drawback to being an OB-GYN nurse is that the entire world tends to believe that because you work with babies all day, that there's nothing in the world you'd prefer to do on a free Saturday night than babysit!

The Pediatric Nurse

It's a small world after all. In pediatrics, you'll be part of the wonderful world of childhood for the second time. If you're lucky, you won't catch all the diseases you missed the first time around.

Pediatrics requires the usual knowledge of anatomy, plus new ways of keeping it still long enough for the doctor to examine it. It also helps to learn to tell a Cabbage Patch doll from a malformed backwoods infant and to spot the difference between a Barbie doll and an uncommunicative, anorexic teenager.

As a pediatric nurse, peace and quiet are what you'll seek, and parents are what you'll avoid. Parents, however, will usually find you, even when you run and hide. "The doctor can answer that better than I can," is the safest answer you can give —even when asked where the doctor himself is. If the waiting room resembles a local playground, you're doing just fine. Just make sure all the furniture is bolted down. Always make sure as well that there is a relatively long wait to see the doctor, so that parents will gratefully accept his prognosis. No matter how serious, it can't be as bad as the waiting room was.

Soon *Sesame Street* and cartoons will filter into your lifestyle. You may amaze your family—and yourself—by your new interest in early-morning TV and novelty breakfast cereals. But do try to keep these secret from your dates, if any.

Scheduling appointments for a pediatrician is slightly more difficult than playing traffic cop at a major intersection during a power failure. Everyone must be next, and the fantasy of selling prime appointments may occur to you, bringing visions of early retirement.

In the hospital pediatrics ward, you're the warden, no matter how many contraband lollipops you give out. You'll feel just like the old woman who lived in a shoe—remember, the one who "had so many children she didn't know what to do"? And she didn't even have to give shots!

Out of frustration you'll find yourself fruitlessly searching a thesaurus for new words or phrases meaning "This will only hurt a little."

No one likes to hurt children, not even a pediatric nurse who's been on duty for ten hours straight and has permanent ear damage. Just keep in mind that kidnapping is illegal, so when you fall in love with a little one, keep repeating to yourself that you just don't have enough bedroom space at home. Of course you could always convert the dining area . . .

The Detox Unit Nurse

Remember Otis from the *Andy Griffith Show?* Otis, the town drunk, checked himself into jail to sleep off his hangovers. If he was your television hero, then the detox unit is for you.

The detox unit is the place where you go when you've had more than one, more times than you can count. Customers check in on the "lay awake 'n' shake" plan, and in the morning they want another shot of whatever substance they choose to abuse, be it liquor or any of the many illegal drugs available on their local street corners. In a pinch your patients will abuse even soft-core drugs such as caffeine or tobacco, so keep a close watch on your coffee cup and pack of butts.

Despite the creepy crawly things your detox patients see on the walls—(sometimes they're there—admit it), some of these patients really are there to dry out. Frustration will have you wishing you could dry them with clothespins and a clothesline—or at least strangle them with same when they start creating self-pitying, con-artist sob stories. Whatever you do, do not listen to these. Do not give patients any unmarked brown paper packages from unidentified visitors.

Instead, do your best to keep their minds off alcohol and drugs. Refrain from referring to a patient's belongings as his "stash," suggesting a game of "gin," or calling the side rails side "bars." If you are planning a vacation to Miami, Colombia, South America, or Queens, New York, refrain from mentioning it.

After listening to their sordid stories of the horrors of addiction, try to convince your patients that the real world of unemployment, violence, and corruption is easier to take without booze or drugs. You might well find yourself worn to a frazzle coping with the volatile temperaments, filthy language, and crazed behavior of your detox patients on a daily basis, but do not give in to the urge to ask them for their sources.

On the other hand, it is important to relax and unwind after your arduous Detox Unit shift. You're only human, so go out, find a bar, find a partner, pour a stiff one, and party.

The Intensive Care Nurse

If your passions in life include video games and the cartoon character Roadrunner, you'll love the beep-beeps of the intensive care unit. As opposed to answering machines, you need not wait for the beeps—they're all around you, as are life-function monitors which may lead you to consider a more relaxing career, such as predicting earthquakes.

This is a nursing area suited to low-keyed but secretly high-strung nurses who are ready to spring into action at a moment's notice. Track shoes may be a worthwhile investment. Being slim is also advisable for the ICU nurse, as you'll often be slithering through an array of machines and equipment greatly

exceeding yourself and your patients in size. Keeping a scorecard might also be in order, as the ICU attracts more medical personnel than you knew were on the floor, in the hospital, or in the city, for that matter.

If you live for the tense final moments of a thriller film where you find yourself sitting at the edge of your seat with no nails left, then intensive care nursing might be for you. The round-the-clock tension offers excitement, and with any luck, just mild insanity. For you prospective ICU nurses, the life-or-death battles are real, and the Grim Reaper does not respect visiting hours.

The Company Nurse

Did you ever dream of working for the FBI or the IRS and having detailed files on everyone at your disposal? If so, you should accept a company nurse position. You'll find yourself the only movable fixture amid a sea of filing cabinets filled to the brim with health and wealth records—facts and data that could make daytime soaps double their ratings.

Since you can't prescribe medication—or advise company employees to go to bed without compromising yourself—your main duty is bandaging injured employees while convincing them that their injuries aren't serious enough to sue the company. Giving out heating pads and aspirin and taking temperatures are some of the challenging parts of your job. Subtle distinctions are important. Remember, a vice-president can take the day off with a 98.7° fever, while secretaries can't be deemed "too sick to work" with less than 103.° The high-spirited elevator operator may be diagnosed as a drunk, but the grouchy old vice-president who passed out on the conference room table reeking of alcohol merely suffered a "dizzy spell."

The politics and rumors of office life will put you in a choice position, you and you alone, will be aware of such vital facts as who has VD, and who will probably be getting it next. Yes, it's the little old office nurse who can suggest to a certain VP that he might prepare to step up a notch simply by sending his higher-up with that heart condition that new secretary with the high skirts and low necklines.

Along these same lines, one important rule to remember is that you must never stay past 5:00 P.M. This assures that you are not a witness to any after-hour escapades (unless, of course, you fancy a healthy executive for your own trysts).

Company nurses need an appreciation for details and a flair for paperwork—by the ton. Keeping track of vital statistics, such as employees' height, weight, blood type, marital status, allergies, how many cars they own, what they eat, how they sleep, and with whom, how many times they've flossed in the past three years, whether they use shampoo with extra body, whether their parents ever had sexual relations near a construction site, and other pertinent facts, is part of your job. Also, making sure employees fill out the proper forms is your responsibility. Forms are essential to anyone needing to leave work for the day, to have his temperature taken, to get a heating pad, to get a form to get a heating pad, to request a form that requests the heating pad form, to say the words "heating pad," to get the vague notion that at some point in life he may need a heating pad, etc., etc. These forms must then be filed in several places, and several ways: last name first, first name last, middle name last, mother's maiden name first, name of next-of-kin behind mother's middle name, and so on. And never ever forget that the social security number must be on everything, including the bandage as you peel it off and the thermometer as you stick it in the patient's mouth. All of this is what we call red tape, and you'll spend more of your time wrapped up in it than in any kind of medical tape.

The office nurse will find herself looking forward to blood drives, fire drills, hostage dramas, and other excuses to get out of her office for a while. It's an ideal compromise position for the nurse who finds herself torn between nursing and business; she can still be in nursing, but with that special corporate touch.

The School Nurse

Many people think school nursing is simply listening to an array of ailments related to upcoming math and English exams. Fortunately, most of the time they're right. But, as racial and economic tensions reach new highs in city schools, the school nurse is beginning to face new challenges. Although you can't do anything major medically for fear of parents, school boards, and lawsuits, the school nurse still has to cope with adolescent Rambos who attach cherry bombs to their bodies, and Mary Lou Retton clones who split their legs, their lips, and their leotards—on the parallel bar.

If you're safely in the suburbs, you may avoid any actual *West Side Story*-style street gang wars (which in real life don't end in carefully choreographed musical numbers). Anywhere else, you may find yourself needing Karate 102 to deal with urban high schoolers. However, even the fearless leader of the Sharks, if he's been cut up enough, can be brought to his knees by the mere odor of an antiseptic swab.

Swallowed crayons, loss of bladder control, and skinned knees are the most common ailments among your average grade-schoolers. Still, there are always one or two kids who'll manage to keep your job interesting by consistently getting into serious accidents or starting major epidemics.

Where inanimate matters are concerned, much of the office nurse routine holds true for the school nurse. As a school nurse, however, you wield far more power; after all, you're an adult —and your patients aren't.

As a school nurse, your files will include 230 letters from "parents" explaining why Sally is allergic to sneakers, Jimmy can't play hockey, Amy can't take gymnastics, Molly can't take showers, and why Zeke has to spend his health classes in the local pizzeria. Essential to your job is the skill of handwriting analysis, so you can tell a forged excuse from the real thing.

Oddly enough, your job includes tending to the teachers as well as the students, even though teachers never get ill in school. (This is why substitute teachers were invented. That way any diagnosis is made *before* the teacher arrives at school and realizes how sick he or she feels.)

The school nurse is a nomad. Teachers smile at you, students make faces, principals nod, and the custodial staff hates your guts. (Hey, is it your fault that kids throw up?) The cafeteria crew is polite (perhaps because

you both wear the same color uniform), but deep down inside, they resent you, too, because they somehow feel that making meatloaf for three hundred kids is a lot harder than weighing them twice a year. Your *true* enemy, however, is the school psychologist. He hates you beyond all reason, because you insist on referring disturbed students to him, instead of curing them yourself with aspirin.

School nursing is ideal for those who enjoy the theater; here is a marvelous opportunity to witness great performances by the thespians of tomorrow. If only you could sell tickets to "The Forty-Five-Minute Stomachache," or the gym class production of "We all Have PMS Today," by the Girls Against Volleyball (for what it does to their nails).

The best thing about the school nurse's job is that you get holidays and plentiful regular vacations (including summers off). Best of all, you never have to work the night shift.

The Floating Nurse

Sally Fields, you may remember, made a habit of taking to the air in *The Flying Nun*. Now, as anyone can tell you, the nurse is first cousin to the sister. True, nurses may not actually have to leave the ground, but they are often required to float, switching from unit to unit and specialty to specialty. As it happens, this is an ideal way to appreciate the hospital architecture, meet a lot of people, get lost frequently, and form no lasting friendships. Yes, one minute you'll be helping a surgeon put in a pacemaker, and a moment later you'll be helping an obstetrician bring out a baby. Also, you'll lose any pesky excess weight running up and down the stairs —in fact, in your constant travels, you may never actually be able to locate the cafeteria.

As the perennial pinch hitter, the floating nurse has to be ready to step in whenever needed—even if it's at the hospital's new annex four hundred miles away. This explains why floating nurses are often tempted to wear white roller skates (for fast unit-to-unit maneuvers) or use old gym class rope-climbing skills to swing out the window of one floor and into the window of another.

Floating from one unit to another can cause confusion. The shrewd floater, can keep an eye out for possible mishaps. When heading from pediatrics to surgery, be careful to avoid handing the surgeon a crayon instead of a clamp. Making the shift from pediatrics to geriatrics may not seem as drastic, but in your confusion, you might find yourself trying to locate a two-year-old's

false teeth—or wearing out an octogenarian with an invigorating game of hide-and-seek.

One thing's for sure, though. As a floating nurse, you may often be confused, but you'll never be bored!

The Soap Opera Nurse

As we all know, soap opera characters spend an inordinate amount of time in the hospital. Soap operas have focused on the lives of many a hospital staff, usually featuring a handsome young doctor or two. Despite this plentitude on television, though, perhaps the most famous soap-opera-type nurse is the one Dustin Hoffman portrayed in *Tootsie*.

On camera, TV soap nurses spend an amazing amount of time at the nurses' station. They also spend a tremendous amount of time talking about their personal lives. For the sake of the ratings, they tend to have numerous affairs with the doctors, residents, patients, and anyone else in the general vicinity. Moreover, when a TV soap nurse goes on duty, she can be seen doing absolutely everything. In one scene she'll be assisting a surgeon, while just moments later she's delivering a baby (in some cases her own). Next she's at the administration desk fending off the press while discussing her upcoming marriage, pending divorce, torrid affair, and life-threatening disease. Naturally she looks ravishing through all of this, with never a hair out of place.

Talk about understaffed hospitals and floating nurses! Off camera is a very different story. Perhaps this sad impression can only be remedied by waiting until a soap opera writer or producer checks into the hospital for emergency surgery. A simple explanation when his call light goes on, saying you can't do anything for him because you've got to get back to the nursing station to finish telling everyone the juicy details of your latest love affair, and the public will be rid of these sorry misimpressions once and for all.

The Supernurse

Look Up in the Sky—
It's a Bird,
It's a Plane,
It's SUPERNURSE!

Able to leap tall doctors in a single bound, it's SUPERNURSE, the ideal of nurses the world over.

Yes, SUPERNURSE can do her rounds, cover for two other nurses, and be at the scene of each and every crisis on floors one through ten while never losing her comforting smile and stiff upper lip. She can be found taking blood in 302 while changing a patient's dressing in 308 at the same time. SUPERNURSE knows the status of every patient in the hospital—and their relatives' conditions as well. She is perky, refreshed and ready to go dancing after a mere twenty-two-hour shift—but not before starting three IVs, giving two dozen shots, and explaining to an upstart intern that she's handled the case he's only read about hundreds of times before.

SUPERNURSE (idol to some, workaholic to others) can be in two or more places at once, can take on any task, no matter how thankless—and always maintains a "good attitude."

SUPERNURSE, wearing a cape with a giant R.N., has been mistakenly straightjacketed and taken to psychiatric time and time again, but she accepts such foul-ups matter-of-factly. No mere mortal, SUPERNURSE does not need to wear a protective apron or retreat to an adjoining room while taking X-rays.

Yes, she's special, made up of tough moral fiber, a stiff backbone, strong arms, and nerves of steel. She also has a heart of gold, and the milk of human kindness runs in her veins. Even so, some doctors do not realize SUPERNURSE's sterling qualities. Others both realize and resent them.

But all nurses worth their salt look up to SUPERNURSE as their inspiration and ideal. (And

inside every nurse, there lurks a
trace—no matter how small—of
SUPERNURSE!)

Nurse's Aides

Who Are They—and Where Are They?

No discussion of nursedom is complete without mentioning these
invaluable accessories. The nurse's aide is a hospital employee who
generally has little or no formal medical education but possesses an
uncanny ability to sense time—break time, lunch time, dinner time,
and quitting time.

Whereas nurses are underpaid and overworked, nurses' aides
make nurses look like billionaires. As your pals, they'll be sure to

let you know it—loud and clear. There's no doubt that they lighten your load, that's for sure—but it'll cost you.

Male nurse's aides are called orderlies (although after listening to them complain about their so-called duties, you'll feel like calling them disorderlies. So do the female aides, who hang out with them on their mutual breaks.) Here is a sample of the exciting opportunities aide-dom offers.

Aides and Orderlies:
A Typical Daily Schedule

1. Serve patients breakfast.
2. Serve their own breakfast.
3. Go to lounge for break.
4. Transport patients to O.R. or physical therapy by gurney or wheelchair.
5. Complain about transporting patients.
6. Take blood pressure and temperature of ward patients.
7. Complain about taking blood pressure and temperature.
8. Take break, smoke, read gossip magazines.
9. Serve patients lunch.
10. Have their own lunch.
11. Complain about lunch.
12. Collect breakfast trays.
13. Go to lounge for coffee and TV break.
14. Order linen and supplies, cigarettes and an afternoon snack.
15. Deliver flowers, distribute mail.
16. Complain about delivering flowers, distributing mail.
17. Collect lunch trays.
18. Complain about collecting lunch trays.
19. Lift one end of patient to help nurse move him.
20. Quote one's duties, giving the exact time limit (in milliseconds) one is allowed to lift a patient.
21. Notice that it's time to leave for the day and drop end of patient.

Naturally this is a stereotypical view of nurse's aides and orderlies. While some do bitch about the "work load," others do exceed their minimum duties out of concern for patients.

The problem is that often nurse's aides undergo training while they're already working. It can be bothersome for the R.N. to have to answer questions like, "Are you sure I'm supposed to do that?" Nurse's aides often feel that you're giving them things to do out of sheer caprice: "I just wanted you to serve these breakfast trays because you had nothing else to do . . . normally the patients don't eat at all." Or, "We don't really have to move this patient—I just wanted you to do some heavy lifting to see if you sweat."

One thing's for sure. If you want to know what time it is, go by the aides' break schedule—you can set your watch by it.

WHAT'S IN A NAME

NURSING INSTRUCTOR:	"Can you name all your patients?"
STUDENT NURSE:	"Why? They already have names."
HEAD NURSE:	"Can you name all your patients?"
OB-GYN NURSE:	"I think the new parents should do that."
HEAD NURSE:	"Can you name all your patients?"
PSYCHIATRIC NURSE:	"Sure, if you count three Napoleons, five George Washingtons, two Ethel Mermans, and a Rambo."

CHAPTER FIVE

How to Succeed in a Hospital Without Even Crying

Patients Are a Virtue

Expecting the Unexpected

Responsibilities You Never Dreamed Of

Along with the important responsibilities you were trained for, such as giving medications, taking blood, keeping patients' charts, etc., you'll soon find yourself charged with "other" responsibilities—ones that were not taught in nursing school.

Here we give you just a few of them:

• Locating lost laundry

• Making a three-hundred pound patient comfortable
• Smuggling in a deli sandwich or slices of pizza for anorexic patients
• Removing Walkman sets from patients who are being wheeled into surgery
• Finding lost dentures and socks
• Making six-foot-long curtains fit a space of approximately twelve feet
• Finding that evasive vase for endless bouquets of wilting flowers
• Ignoring that one visitor too many
• Waking up on-duty residents who are dead to the world
• Fine-tuning patients' TV sets
• Refereeing wheelchair races

- Disturbing the patient without making the bed

a patient is on the way. Actually this step is where you adjust the lights, window blinds, set the temperature, etc. (One might almost get the impression from the manual's description that with a little soft music you'll be all set for a romantic candlelight supper.)

2. OPEN BED

Critically ill patients may have a difficult time doing this for themselves, so the manual has decided to remind you of this step. Generally a closed bed provides less comfort and movability. Also, you should turn back the covers and fluff the pillows (which you will learn from the manual are to be found in the bed upon opening it). Lowering the bed also helps, so that patients don't have to take a flying leap to gain access.

Preparing for a New Patient

The following three steps were adapted (and critically reviewed) from an actual nurses' manual. (Honest!)

1. PREPARE ROOM

Initially, one might think this is where you inform the room that

3. PLACE A GOWN ON THE BED

Go with something informal, no scratchy or slippery silk. Presumably, nursing etiquette is very delicate in this case and the mere presence of the gown on the bed is enough of a hint for the patient to remove his street clothes and don said gown. Hopefully, if the patient is unconscious, the nurse will aid in the transference of the gown from bed to patient's body.

Who's the Boss?

Establishing Patient-Nurse Relations

Most patients, at least those who are conscious and/or in their right minds, feel anxious when they first enter a hospital, and your first job is to make them feel at ease. As you escort a new hospital inmate to his or her room, always call the patient by his or her real name. This can be easily ascertained by glancing at the patient's admittance file, since he or she won't have a chart yet.

Smile pleasantly and tell the patient, "I'm Miss Adams, the nurse assigned to take care of you." (If your name isn't Adams, use your own name. This will prevent the patient from becoming confused by so many Nurse Adamses running around the place.)

Maintain a pleasant, positive attitude as you show the patient around his twelve-foot-by-six-foot cubicle, pointing out such reassuring features as the call button (to be used for dire emergencies only), the side rails on the bed, and the stainless steel bedpan. Try and make the patient feel at home. This should be easy if he or she is used to living in a sterile white environment and using rubbing alcohol as a room freshener.

In your limited time (about three minutes), acquaint the patient with hospital rules, equipment, and routine. Let your patients know from the outset what you'll be doing for them, with them, and to them during their hospital stay. Gently remind them over and over again who is really in charge, in case any lingering delusions of free will prevail.

Most patients will feel comfortable in your capable hands. Some may need reassuring, it is true, while still others will require a severe blow to the head with a blunt instrument. With any luck, you will immediately establish a good rapport with your patients. If luck doesn't work, be extremely polite; if that doesn't work, you may have to resort to begging or threatening. But be subtle. Sometimes holding a large syringe in hand while talking to new or obstreperous patients can be quite effective.

Still, no matter how firm and fair you are, some patients will act up, making your job even more impossible than it already is. There are days when it may seem difficult to keep your temper in check, and your hands to yourself in the face of patients' flagrant flouting of hospital rules, your authority, and the rights of their fellow patients.

Nevertheless, if you want to keep your job, you must keep your cool 99 percent of the time. *Understatement* is the key. Learn to convert shrieking curses into sweet suggestions, dire threats into gentle persuasion—before the words ever leave your mouth.

Use a reverse rule of thumb when dealing with difficult patients: the more bizarre their behavior, the more reasonable your reactions should be.

Nurse Knows Best

What to Say to Impossible Patients

- "How would it be if we turned the television set down just a little, so that the people in the housing project across the street can get some sleep. You wouldn't mind that, would you?"
- "Perhaps Mr. Johnson would prefer it if *I* took his temperature. Why not just hand me the thermometer and climb back into your own bed? But thanks for trying to help."
- "Please try to refrain from tap dancing up and down the halls, as it is getting late."
- "How about if we close the window, untie these bed sheets, and you stay here just for tonight. Okay?"
- "Perhaps your roommate would prefer it if you didn't go through his personal belongings. Since he can't get out of bed, why don't we just put his watch back in the drawer?"
- "Oh dear, how did these brussels sprouts get all over the floor? Now, would you like another dish of them, or would you rather pick them up and keep these for souvenirs?"

Types of Patients . . . Who Try Your Patience

Patients range from the sublime to the slime, but without them your job just wouldn't be the same—in fact, it wouldn't exist at all. Here are some common types of hospital patients and their peculiarities.

THE SLAVE DRIVER

Some patients insist that you do just one thing to make them comfortable. After all, it's your job to care for them, and they'll only be comfortable if you're constantly making them that way.

THE SPOILED SLAVE DRIVER

Usually women with maids, these ladies are always satisfied while you're doing something for them, but never satisfied when you leave. Thus, they'll call you back to do everything for them all over again.

THE PUSH BUTTON PLAYER

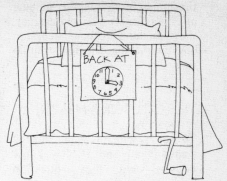

Often children or curious adults, these patients can't get over the amazing fact that if they press the call button, a nurse will show up, magically, again and again. These people also drive stewardesses crazy, and often pull the emergency cord on a train just to see if it will stop.

THE GUILT SPECIALIST

Bold as brass, these patients will try and do your job for you—then make you feel incompetent. You'll hear things like, "Oh, I took my own temperature and gave myself a bath. I didn't want to wake you."

THE YENTA

They want to know you personally, dear. These patients inquire about your health, your age, your social life, whether you have a boyfriend, a sex life, etc. Their concern seems touching until you realize they're either bucking for special treatment or gathering information for future blackmail.

THE WANDERER

This type of patient likes to roam around. They're never in one place for long—especially bed. They "float" from floor to floor . . . and it's your job to find them.

THE ECCENTRIC

Some patients like to sing at odd hours; others give vent to an occasional primal scream; and still others like to tell jokes—especially dirty ones. Sometimes these favorite pastimes are just not appropriate to a hospital—like visiting other patients at 4:00 A.M., putting whoopie cushions in wheelchairs, and telling pre-op patients the one about the two quack doctors who did this operation.

THE PLAYBOY

Usually middle-aged, balding married men who've seen *The Sensuous Nurse*, playboy patients have all the lines you don't want to hear. As they're looking for very personal care, these men often mistake medical attention for stimulation. In fact, they mistake eating, sleeping, and everything else for stimulation.

THE DOCTOR'S HELPER

These patients assume M.D.'s know it all and R.N.'s know nothing—and they question your authority constantly. "Why are you emptying my bedpan—did the doctor tell you to do that? Lunch? Did the doctor say I can eat? Is this the food he said I should eat? Are you sure?" They prefer to fire their constant barrage of questions at the doctor himself, but since M.D.'s are famous for their lightning-fast rounds, you're the one who's stuck with them.

Patients can be wonderful and appreciative; they can also be a pain the the neck. You'll get your share of both varieties during your nursing career.

Off the Record

A Look at Nurses' Notes on Some Very Well-Known Patients

On Hugh Hefner: "A feminist nurse stuck a staple in his navel."

On Johnny Carson: "It was weird, but suddenly one week Gary Shandling was in bed instead of him."

On Don Johnson: "It was the first time I ever had to wait in line to give a sponge bath."

On Joan Crawford: "We were careful to remove all the coat hangers from her closet."

On Liberace: "Every time I'd put down the dinner tray I was sure I'd knock over the candelabra and set the room on fire!"

On Sybil: "Sixteen dinners, sixteen baths—it was ridiculous!"

On John Holmes: "The poor nursing student took one look and fainted dead away."

On Howard Hughes: "Was he here?"

On Ted Turner: "What can I say? He wanted the best of care, so he bought the hospital."

On Loretta Swit: "Poor dear, she was so confused. I must have explained to her twenty times that *we* were the nurses and *she* was the patient."

On Vanessa Williams: "She wanted exclusive rights to her X-rays. Who could blame her, poor thing."

On Madonna: "It took five orderlies to prep her for her operation!"

On Don Rickles: "Talk about nasty! It got to the point where we were putting soiled sheets on his bed!

Giving Medication

The Unwritten Rules

Every nurse learns that the unwritten rulebook is heftier than the manual. Here is just a sampling:

1. Make sure the medication is appropriately labeled, not by the patient, and not in lipstick or Magic Marker.
2. Be sure you're giving medication to the proper patient and not the one who's begging for it.
3. Never give an injection, or shot, in the dark.
4. Never slip an unwilling patient his or her medication in a tuna sandwich.
5. Never slip medication into a bitchy head nurse's coffee, especially if she's a tea drinker.
6. Never give in to patients' entreaties for you to "try it first."
7. When giving injections, never hit the patient's bone, nerve, visitors, or flowers.
8. Never grind up a pill by putting it on the floor and stepping on it—at least not while other people are around.
9. Never give doggie bags of medication to patients leaving the hospital.
10. Never given injections to more than one person at the same time.
11. Never replace hospital remedies with chicken soup, unless the doctor orders it.

Just What the Doctor Ordered

Fast Food vs. Hospital Food

What with specimens, bedpans, escorted trips to the bathroom, blood tests, enemas, etc., the nurse has a large part to play in what's coming out of the patients—including verbal abuse. Therefore, the nurse should justifiably be in charge of what goes into them. For some reason, though, she is not. It's the doctor who orders food for the patients. The nurse's job is to see that special orders don't upset them, which isn't easy, since they rarely get to have it their way.

Whereas in most hospitals the nurse's aide actually delivers the food, *you* have to see that it's right and explain to the patient why his or her order of clams on the half shell has been changed to Jell-o in the half cup.

It's *your* job to see that friends and relatives don't bring in rolled-up copies of *Sports Illustrated* with a salami hero tucked inside. You must guard against the old fries-in-the-bedroom-slipper trick, not to mention the malted-in-the-flower-vase routine. Patients, like everybody else, crave their favorite foods, and it's not surprising that most of them prefer fast foods to strained foods.

Special Diets

We Try Not to Let Them Upset Us

Clear Liquid Diet

This includes anything you can see through—the IV bottle, broth, apple juice, Perrier, ginger ale, and plain old water. These are ideal for the paranoid patient to let him or her see for sure that you're not putting anything in his or her "food."

Semiliquid Diet

Cream soups, pabulum, applesauce, yogurt, and pudding are featured on this diet, which is ideally suited to six-month-old infants. Is it any wonder that adult patients often throw this fare in nurses' faces?

Soft Diet

Ideal for the patient whose dentures you can't locate, the soft diet consists of any food which, when placed in the palm of the hand and squeezed, will ooze out between your fingers. Grits, soft-boiled eggs, mashed potatoes and bananas, tapioca pudding, and anything gummy that can be gummed are the featured items.

Light Diet

This consists of foods that don't weigh enough to stay down on a plate, such as Jell-o, dry toast, spinach soufflé, scrambled eggs, and lemon meringue pie. Unfortunately, this diet does not include light beer.

Heavy Diet

A diet consisting of foods so heavy that the patient can't get out of bed. Anything with cement, wood fiber, or glue in it, such as hospital bakery products and gravy, fits this group.

Doctor's Diet

Strangely enough, it consists of all the rich foods his or her patients are told to avoid, such as filet mignon, cheeseburgers, home fries, stuffed pork chops, spaghetti Alfredo, eggs Benedict (Arnold), chocolate soufflé, and before, after, and during drinks.

Visiting Mom's Diet

This unordered and unauthorized diet consists of an endless variety of delicious homemade dishes which these patients' doting Mamas prepare for their ailing darlings and then bring to the hospital two or three times a day. They are then promptly confiscated by vigilant doctors and nurses. Dishes that come highly recommended and for-bidden (to patients) include: chicken soup with matzoh balls; barbecued ribs with black-eyed peas; lasagna, sausages, and pepper; and enchiladas and tacos with refried beans.

Regulation Hospital Diet

This is usually the most diffi-cult one to swallow. It includes all foods that can be ordered from the hospital menu and are cooked in mass quantity without benefit of season or seasoning, until the original color, flavor, fiber, and consistency are totally destroyed. Surprisingly, a large number of patients who are on this diet recover sufficiently to leave the hospital.

Nurse's Diet

So much for the patients. Now, how about yourself? Nurses learn fast to live on food that stays in the stomach and doesn't return easily when run-ning from room to room. Foods eaten prior to work should not be memorable. (Do you really want to reexperience digging lobster from the shell while help-ing a surgeon remove tissue from an infected kneecap?)

Cold foods are a good idea, since you may doze off while waiting for hot ones to cook. Get used to chemicals and preserva-tives, since you will have to rely

on foods that won't go bad be-tween the time you order them and the time you finally get to eat them (often hours—or even days—later).

Coffee: Your Key to Survival

If you don't drink coffee, you'd better stock up on those extra-large bottles of "Classic Coke:" you're going to need *something* to keep you awake.

The average nurse drinks any-where from eight to thirty- eight cups of coffee a day—and that's just to get through her shift. Stu-dent nurses drink even more, and during finals, coffee IV's are commonplace.

If you OD on caffeine, mar-tinis or massive quantities of wine are effective antidotes.

TIPS ON FEEDING A PATIENT

- Forget the old train-in-the-tunnel approach.
- Never sterilize a utensil by heating it to 300 degrees just prior to putting it in the pa-tient's mouth.
- Don't cut corners by using feed bags—even if the pa-tient does eat like a horse.
- Cut food before putting it in the patient's mouth—not after.

Tint, Color, and Vertical Hold

The Nurse's TV Guide

To Florence Nightingale's advantage, television had not yet been invented during her nursing career. Unfortunately, the modern nurse often finds her nerves strained in the attempt to adjust patients' TV sets in time for *Dynasty, Dallas,* or *The Bill Cosby Show.*

Here are some pertinent TV facts that may help:

1. Most modern televisions come with digital-tuning, fine-tuning, and color-tuning adjustments. Hospital televisions, on the other hand, come with just one knob for tuning everything—and an antenna that resembles a tuning fork. Thus, your job as a TV repairman is made much simpler.
2. The hospital television set is generally located at the end of a long cranelike object designed to be: hard to reach without pulling a muscle or tearing pantyhose; ready to swing down and strike an unsuspecting nurse on her head.
3. The object of bringing TV into patients' rooms is for their entertainment. As it turns out, the entertainment usually comes from watching you standing on a chair, stretching your left arm up to hold the antenna at a forty-seven-degree angle, and your right arm up to turn the knob while trying to pull your skirt down at the same time. The problem is compounded when the head nurse walks in and accuses you of putting on a strip-tease show.
4. If your problems with servicing patients' TV sets reach a crisis point, you can always make up a batch of hand-lettered out-of-order signs and hang them on the antennas. Then follow through by "pulling the plug."

Dealing with Hard-core TV Addicts

Sometimes convincing the patient that he or she can survive

without Don Johnson, J.R. Ewing, *Monday Night Football,* or *General Hospital* is more difficult than reassuring them before major surgery that they "won't miss" the organ in question, as illustrated by the following dialogue:

NURSE: "Your chart shows that you're doing much better today, Mrs. Redbone."

PATIENT: "I don't care about that—I want to see *All My Children.*"

NURSE: "I'm sure all your children will visit you later today."

PATIENT: "I don't mean *them*— I mean my soap!"

NURSE: "Well, then, we'll give you a bath in just a little while."

PATIENT: "I don't want a bath —I want my daytime serial!"

NURSE: "Oh, good, you're geting your appetite back. I'll go order more cereal right away."

PATIENT: "No, no, no, damn it! I just want to watch my soap opera on the television set!"

In the Nurse's Pocket(s)

Pens: Several of various colors for various charts—and be-

cause doctors, residents, and everyone else in the hospital will borrow them . . . permanently.

Tape: Two rolls, one transparent and one surgical.

Scissors: Essential for trying to start rolls of tape and for trimming your perpetually brokken nails.

Alcohol preps: To be used for giving injections—and for rubbing on yourself when perspiration has triumphed over deodorant or perfume.

Needle: Having already used it, there's no reason in hell why it's there other than for your absurd scrapbook or hospital memorabilia, or to prove to your kids that you *do* give injections.

Change purse: Be certain to carry more change than you did last week, as vending machine prices go up weekly.

Note pad: Entries range from illegible scribbles to notes for your future nursing novel. You'll probably also find last week's shopping list, which included a present for your mom's birthday, which was five days ago.

Tourniquet: Just in case you can't wake up the exhausted intern on duty when someone decides to hemorrhage.

Tissues: For the winter cold you'll never get enough rest to get over.

One button: A small reminder of your neglected family. It fell off your son's baseball jacket last summer, and you hope to have it sewn back on in time for Little League's spring training.

Rules of the Game

Gimme a Break!

A Dozen Things You'll Have Time to Do on Your "Free" Time During Shift

1. Inhale.
2. Get a spoon of yogurt halfway to your mouth.
3. Bend your knees in an effort to sit.
4. Put the first quarter into the vending machine.
5. Read the first two words of the newspaper's headline.
6. Exhale.
7. Put lipstick on your upper lip.
8. Sneeze once.
9. Plan the first thirty seconds of your day off.
10. Dial the first digits of your home phone to see how your kids are.
11. Open a can of soda.
12. List the first item on your grocery list.

Plan in advance, and choose one, because it's all you'll have time for.

Foot-in-Mouth Disease

Two Dozen Things You May Wish You Didn't Have to Say, or Ask

1. "Whose urine specimen is this?"
2. "Must the entire defensive front line visit you at the same time?"
3. "I could have sworn my shift ended forty minutes ago."
4. "Are you sure that's all it comes to after taxes?"
5. "Could we change that date to a Tuesday morning?"
6. "Why isn't resident a four-letter word?"
7. "Are you sure this is real food?"
8. "What do you mean, you didn't reach the bedpan in time?"
9. "Why is Mr. Peterson hiding in the broom closet?"
10. "Sleep? What's sleep?"
11. "What do you mean, meet you in O.R. at midnight?!"
12. "You wouldn't mind if I wore roller skates on my rounds, would you?"
13. "The aspirins? They're for me."
14. "What do you mean, the baby's missing?"
15. "Why is Mr. Peterson hiding in the elevator?"
16. "I hope this kid had rabies shots."

Hospital Procedures:
A Short Quiz

1. If you need a light bulb changed you:

    (A) Call Con Edison

    (B) Call maintenance and then buy a lantern to use while waiting for them.

    (C) Change it yourself.

2. Hospital calls should be transferred to another department by:

    (A) The hospital operator.

    (B) The telephone company.

    (C) Satellite.

    (D) You.

3. Lost items should be taken to:

    (A) The lost and found department.

    (B) The nearest police precinct.

    (C) The gift shop for resale.

    (D) Your house.

4. After filling out a work repair request you:

    (A) Keep the original copy.

    (B) Take two aspirin.

    (C) Say a prayer.

    (D) Buy a hammer and get to work.

17. "I called housekeeping six hours ago."
18. "No, Doctor, it's his *right* shoulder."
19. "What do you mean, you've never been to the third floor?"
20. "Why is Mr. Peterson hiding in the nurses' station?"
21. "No, I did not star in *The Sensuous Nurse!*"
22. "I'll bet Florence never had to contend with computers!"
23. "No, Doctor, the room isn't swaying."
24. "Cherry Ames certainly *was* fiction!"

So You Think You've Got a Bright Idea . . .

In nursing, as in any other profession, there are generally systematic, tried-and-true methods of dealing with problems. But every now and then a solution will turn up that really doesn't make sense. And at those times, a nurse just might get a clever, innovative idea about a new and better way to do something—in short, a brainstorm . . . But will others appreciate your genius?

Here's a list of the twenty-five most common reactions you can expect to get in response to a bright idea:

1. It's against hospital policy.
2. It's not practical.
3. It's never been done before.
4. It'll cost too much.
5. The administration will never allow it.
6. The doctors won't like it.
7. The union won't like it.
8. The maintenance staff won't like it.
9. The mayor won't like it.
10. The cast of *General Hospital* won't like it.
11. Japanese midget wrestler living in Boston won't like it.
12. It's too radical.
13. It's too feminist.
14. It's communistic.
15. If we do it, then every hospital will have to.
16. You've been working here too long.
17. You've been hanging around the mental ward too long.
18. It's that kind of thinking that starts wars.
19. It was done in Belgium in 1928 and it didn't work.
20. It was done in Rome in 1624 and it doesn't work.
21. It's not tax deductible.
22. It's a good idea, but not for us.
23. It's a great idea—I'm glad I thought of it.
24. If we do it, the hospital will collapse.
25. You're not getting paid for bright ideas.

LEGAL IMPLICATIONS AND YOU, THE NURSE
A Quiz

1. Professional Negligence:

    (A) Can be considered a criminal act.
    (B) Is what professional women sleep in.
    (C) Is what spouses of professionals claim in divorce suits.

2. If an adult patient cannot, for some reason, sign a consent form:

    (A) A spouse or other designated person can sign for him.
    (B) An orderly or gift shop employee can sign for him.
    (C) You have to fill in the *X* for him.

3. A nurse who engages in activities beyond the legally recognized scope of nursing:

    (A) Stands an excellent chance of winning the Florence Nightingale Golden Thermometer award.

(B) Runs the risk of having to marry the patient because of complex tribal customs.

(C) Can be held criminally negligent and may have stripes added to her white outfit.

(D) Can be promoted to honorary doctor.

4. "Battery" is:

(A) The intentional, unauthorized touching of another person.

(B) The unintentional touching of another's person.

(C) The intentional touching of another person's person.

(D) Duracell or Eveready's leading money-maker.

5. Which is *not* an act of false imprisonment?

(A) Locking a healthy patient of sound mind in a storage closet.

(B) Locking a patient's unruly visitors in a storage closet.

(C) Locking a flirtatious doctor in a storage closet.

(D) Locking a homicidal escaped mental patient carrying a machete in a storage closet.

6. Which constitutes invasion of privacy?

(A) Selling a patient's medical files to the *National Enquirer*.

(B) Allowing Bob Guccione to photograph female patients in hopes that someday they'll be elected Miss America.

(C) Leading hospital tour groups through patients' rooms at all hours of the day and night.

(D) All of the above.

7. Slander occurs when:

(A) You call the man on the window ledge a nutcase when he's planning to jump.

(B) You call the man on the window ledge a nutcase when he's actually a sniper.

(C) You call the man on the window ledge a nutcase and he turns out to be a window-washer.

8. Medical records are:

(A) Hospital property.

(B) The next best thing to reading personal diaries.

(C) Popular albums recorded by patients in the shower.

(D) To be sent immediately to the CIA, FBI, and IRS.

The Doctor and You

The Total Doctor

The total doctor operates on the principle that God was created in his or her image. He or she maintains a consistent manner and appearance which seem to say, "I'm calm, in control and dignified," but really mean, "I'm paying an enormous amount of malpractice insurance, don't have all the answers they think I do, can't find my way around the hospital, don't know if the opposite sex is attracted to me because of myself or because I'm a doctor, can't help slicing to the right with my 3 iron, and need a nurse to keep my head screwed on straight—but no one must ever know these things. . . ."

In an earlier incarnation, the total male doctor was the total resident, operating under the misguided impression that every nurse not only idolized him but couldn't wait her turn. Unfortunately, if in fact you love someone who has become a doctor, you'll usually have to take third place behind both (a) his narcissism (self-love) and (b) his mother's love and admiration of him.

Doctors worked hard to get through med school, and they'll never let you forget it. They also earn good incomes (and their mothers will never let you forget it). Face it; they are more intelligent than all other people, even in areas they know nothing about.

Doctors carry credit cards in order not to part with "real money" too frequently, but they'll always let it be known when they've spent huge amounts. (After all, it *is* hard to miss the new Mercedes parked in the hospital lobby.) Doctors also carry beepers so they can be contacted anywhere at any time and run to the nearest telephone to immediately call a nurse to handle the situation.

Yes, doctors do play golf. Why? Because it's one of the few things they can't get a resident, intern, or nurse to do *for* them.

The female of the species has surmounted insurmountable obstacles. The woman doctor is not only your superior—she's superior to the rest of humanity as well. She's got *both* parents bragging about her. She's made an indelible mark on the history of the world. Love, marriage, family, social life, the arts, and a sense of humor are trite and trivial pursuits compared to her career.

The most amazing facts about M.D.'s are:

- How after med school, internship, and residency, the long hours and hard work of their career are largely over.

- How they keep from falling off their pedestals.
- How they can work without breaking loose from their own embrace.

Where's the Doctor?

Answers to This Age-Old Question

In the daytime, the possibilities are endless. The doctor can be at his office, in the operating room, or at the clinic—golf clinic, that is, correcting a drastic slice with his 3 wood. Other alternatives include the possibility that the doctor is shy and can't face people wearing hospital gowns, or that he is home in bed with a bad cold. Any of these explanations will do when confronting an inquisitive patient during the daytime. At night, however, explaining that a doctor often sleeps and sees his or her family is out of the question. Patients don't like to think of their godlike idols in such humdrum terms. Therefore it's up to you to create new and fascinating explanations of where the doctor could be. Tell them that he suddenly flew to Hollywood to perform an emergency facelift for a famous star —sure, that's it—or to audition for a role in *St. Elsewhere*.

Patients look up to doctors— they have to, because they're lying flat on their backs in bed. Nevertheless, convincing a patient that he or she doesn't really need the doctor may be the most effective way of answering the question, especially when half of the time you'll be correct.

Conversation Between Diligent Nurse and Distracted Doctor

NURSE: Excuse me . . .

DOCTOR (on telephone): Yes, but if we tee off at nine-thirty it'll be too crowded on the fairway!

NURSE: Excuse me . . .

DOCTOR: Hold on a second, Mark . . . what is it?

NURSE: Mrs. Adams in 229 is complaining of pains in her right abdominal region.

DOCTOR: Tell her I'll be right there. *(On telephone.)* Look Mark, I gotta run, I've got a . . . no, I don't want to play at Westwood Country Club. The course is too slow . . . because I played there last year . . . I'm telling you . . .

NURSE: Excuse me, doctor . . .

DOCTOR: Yes. Yes . . . just a second . . .

NURSE: Well, I hate to bother you, but I'm fairly certain it's her appendix. I checked her white blood cell count and it's very low.

DOCTOR: Thank you, nurse, I'll be right there. Okay, Mark, really I gotta get . . . Sam!? I don't want him as the fourth! He spends half the day looking for balls he's sliced into the trees. I know Westwood doesn't have trees, but I don't like the course. It's muddy . . . every place you hit it, the ball gets dirty.

NURSE: Excuse me, Doctor, but I'm gonna prep her for an appendectomy. What's the first step?

DOCTOR: You have to wash the balls.

NURSE: I have to what!? We're talking about Mrs. Adams here, Doctor!

DOCTOR: Hold it, Mark. Did you ask me something?

NURSE: Yes, I'm prepping Mrs. Adams for an appendectomy.

DOCTOR: Wait a second Mark, I'm talking to someone here. They never leave me alone . . . um, listen, use your judgment and I'll be in in just a second.

NURSE: Yes, but she's . . .

DOCTOR: Relax, relax, everyone gets so frantic around here. We should all calm down a little . . . Mark, I really have to be going . . . I'll . . . NO!

I'M NOT LETTING SAM BORROW MY FOUR IRON! I DON'T EVEN WANT HIM COMING ALONG!

(Later that afternoon.)

DOCTOR: Yeah, but if you pick up Jeff first, we could tee off at eight-thirty, which would give us . . .

NURSE: Excuse me, Doctor, excuse me.

DOCTOR: Just a second, Mark . . . what is it?

NURSE: I just finished surgery on Mrs. Adams, and she's in recovery doing fine.

DOCTOR: Okay, great . . . that's great . . . listen Mark, I've gotta run, one of my nurses is working her pretty little head off, yeah, she just did surg . . . SHE JUST DID WHAT!? *(Hangs up phone.)*

NURSE: Would you like to see Mrs. Adams?

DOCTOR: Yes, she *is* my patient. Who did you assist in the operating room?

NURSE: Assist?

DOCTOR: Are you trying to tell me that you . . .?

NURSE: And was commended by the chief surgeon, who was busy at the time.

DOCTOR: Mrs. Adams . . . are you all right? My God, you poor wom . . . no, don't thank me . . . you just rest . . . well, of course you didn't feel a thing. You were under anaesthesia, I hope . . . I mean of course, and had an experienced medical staff in there . . . yes, I've done plenty of them, and you know . . . yours was a simple operation, nothing especially memorable to me . . . yes I know it's hard to talk. You just rest . . . Nurse, get Mrs. Adams some juice! Nurse!

NURSE (On telephone.): Mark, just tell me where he keeps his clubs! I only need one, I have to practice teeing off—on his head!

The Trouble with Residents:

Problems and Solutions

PROBLEM: Residents refuse to believe that you've been at the hospital longer and know your way around better than they do.
SOLUTION: Wheel a sleeping resident to the farthest part of the hospital and see if he can find his way back.

PROBLEM: Residents always sleep when on duty, but complain when their names are paged.

SOLUTION: Wheel sleeping resident up against the P.A. system and have him snore into the microphone.

PROBLEM: Residents attempt to belittle you in front of your superiors.
SOLUTION: Wheel a sleeping resident outside and deposit him in the chief administrator's car.

PROBLEM: Residents refuse to acknowledge you might be right in suspecting that there's something wrong with a patient. You: "He doesn't look right to me." Resident: "Oh, it's just the lighting in here."
SOLUTION: Paint a sleeping resident green and tell him, "It's just the lighting."

PROBLEM: Foreign residents treat you like a second-class citizen.
SOLUTION: Put a sleeping foreign resident in your car, drive him to the airport, and send him back to his own country . . . second class.

PROBLEM: Residents continuously try to get fresh and seduce you and all the other nurses.
SOLUTION: Tuck feminine undergarments in a sleeping resident's pockets, so when he groggily responds to a page, he'll have bras and frilly panties dangling from his person.

The Fine Distinctions

What Does R.N. Really Stand For?

Have you been confused about the meaning of R.N. since you finished becoming one? Do you find that other people think it actually means something other than what it does?

- Have you thought it might stand for *Really Nuts?*
- Do your patients think it stands for *Real Nice?*
- Does your head nurse think you're *Real Nervous?*
- Do doctors think it stands for *Right Now?*
- If you catch colds a lot does it stand for *Running Nose?*
- After twelve years of being overworked, does your therapist consider you *Really Neurotic?*
- Do nearsighted patients and ex-sailors think you're from the *Royal Navy?*
- After a long, hard day, are you sometimes mistaken for *Richard Nixon?*
- Do short people dislike you and does L.A. love you because they think you're *Randy Newman?*
- does L.P.N. also mean *Lousy Pay Nursing* or that you *Look Pretty Neat?*

Ten Things to Wonder About Visitors

1. Why do people show up who haven't seen the patient in six months and say things like, "You look terrible?"
2. Why do visitors bring cigarettes to someone with lung disease?
3. Why do visitors break into long stories about the article they read in the newspaper concerning the surgeon who left his wallet inside the patient's small intestine?
4. Why do relatives discuss other relatives who died of the same ailment the patient's in for, even if the patient is twelve and "poor old Aunt Erma" was ninety-three?
5. Why, after only ten minutes, do visitors get hungry? And why, in spite of your explicit directions, can't they find the cafeteria?
6. Why do visitors of single male patients (mothers and male friends especially) comment on how adorable the nurse is while you're standing right there?
7. Why do visitors seem to think you know all the intimate details of doctors' personal lives—even their whereabouts?
8. Why do male visitors want to discuss *your* anatomy instead of the patient's?

9. Why do visitors ask loud, personal questions about the patient in the other bed?
10. Why do visitors spend more time at the nurses' station than they do with the patient?

ARE YOU THE DOCTOR?
How to Tell M.D.'s from R.N.'s

With the rising number of female doctors and male nurses, sometimes telling the difference between M.D.'s and R.N.'s can be a bit of a problem. Thus we have a list of ways for patients and new hospital staff members to tell who's who.

M.D.'s:	R.N.'s:
Show concern with your hospital coverage.	Show concern with your hospital comfort.
Will leave you a written note or prescription.	Will translate the doctor's hieroglyphics.
Admit patients to the hospital.	Can actually *find* the patients once they're in the hospital.
Wear Rolex watches, and vacation in Europe and other exotic areas of the world	Wear Timex watches and vacation in the forty-eight states (Alaska and Hawaii are too expensive).
Carry a beeper so that if they're needed, they'll be present.	Are omnipresent.
Are never in their office on Wednesdays.	Explain to disgruntled patients why the doctor's not in on Wednesdays.
Misplace surgical instruments.	Take the blame.

Creative Disasters 101

So You Think *You've* Had Bad Days

One Nurse's Story

The day started out with the patient in room 239 returning breakfast moments after finishing it. Then I learned that the nurse's aides not only have a union, but they're five minutes away from a strike. Suddenly I began to appreciate their efforts more, especially when I attempted to lift the guy in 243, whose weight just happened to match his room number. We're both sweating and straining when disaster strikes and the young, blue-eyed student nurse knocks the room partition onto me—and Mr. 243.

After order is restored, we bid the aides farewell and correct a few spelling errors on their picket signs. But the day is not a total delight, as elderly Mr. Cohen in 247 seems to have vanished. As we search for our wandering patient, I just happen to smell smoke, followed almost immediately by a loud scream. Lo and behold, if the little teen sex queen in 353 hasn't gone and broken the "No Smoking" rule in a big way—she's caught her hair on fire. Thinking quickly, we play volunteer fire department and rescue her before too much damage is done to her Cyndi Lauper hairstyle. And if she's not getting the most attention of the day, Mr. Big in 231 is. He's got a few policemen visiting to ask him questions, but since he's not in shape to answer them, I end up policing the police while praying that this doesn't mean I'm an accessory to whatever he did or tried to do that got him here in the first place.

At this point, having found our misplaced elder thanks to screams from Gynecology, I foolishly figure a simple sponge bath will offer a respite from the hectic pace. Little do I know that bathing Mr. 240 will "uncover" another Mr. Big. He accompanies his physical arousal with a few verbal suggestions, and maintaining my best bedside manner, I remind him that he needs his rest and his strength, while I try reminding myself why I bothered waking up this morning.

Now back at the nurses' station, I'm off my feet for a little while. Lucky me, I'm down on all fours cleaning up a spilled specimen cup thanks to a collision with a half-awake resident. But the big question of the morning comes on my rounds to room 349, where we wonder what Dr. Armstrong has written for the proper medication . . . is this 62, or 6.2 units?

"Finally, finding Dr. Armstrong on a Wednesday, on the fourth hole, and enduring his wrath of being disturbed, we're set to give medication and moments later set out to find lost dentures—without the help of an aide. During my quest for the disappearing dentures, I just happen to glance up at the clock, noting four important facts . . .

1. It's only 11:20 A.M.
2. Hospital clocks are always correct
3. The day is not even half over
4. I'm never going to make it through this one!

Hospital Hazards

In the hustle and bustle of a busy hospital, injuries and accidents are bound to happen. Fortunately, there's a doctor in the house. Unfortunately, he may be hard to find.

The most common hospital injuries were found to be sprains, strains, and puncture wounds. There are many types of hospital injuries, however, and the key question is not what are they, but how do they occur?

Here are some common injuries and the ways in which they usually occur:

1. Back strain from lifting a 290-pound patient with an orderly who's using just one hand while busily checking his watch for "coffee break time."

2. Being bitten by patients while attempting to take their temperatures.
3. Head injuries from being struck by flying objects such as lunch trays, bedpans, and flower arrangements.
4. Being burned when attempting to confiscate marijuana or other cigarettes.
5. Breaking your hand while pounding an answer into a doctor's head.
6. Losing two or three teeth while trying to inject a patient with an extremely powerful left hook.
7. Loss of hearing from working too close to the P.A. system.
8. Being trampled by reporters seeking access to famous patients.
9. Having your feet run over up by souped-up wheelchairs.
10. Spraining an ankle jumping for joy when your vacation begins.
11. Breaking your foot by kicking the resident who had you race up four flights of stairs to answer an "emergency question" you answered a half hour earlier.
12. Stab wounds from assisting during the new surgeon's first operation.
13. Strained back from lifting a fainted father in the delivery room.
14. Developing a neck twitch from a head nurse who's always looking over your shoulder.

15. Stomach disorders from living on hospital food and black coffee.
16. Amnesia from being so overworked that you've forgotten your own name.
17. Shoulder strain from waiting for an IV holder and playing Statue of Liberty with the bag for twenty minutes.

Hospital Film Festival

Some New "In-Service" Nursing Releases

Nurses are required to watch films that inform them of the latest trends and new developments in hospital methods and equipment. None of these films feature Clint Eastwood, or even a cameo by Robert Redford, and as you watch them you'll be taking notes, not eating popcorn.

Here are some of the latest films released to hospitals around the country:

★★★★★★★★★★★★★★★★★★★★★★★★★★
YOU TAKE MY BREATH AWAY
★★★★★★★★★★★★★★★★★★★★★★★★★★

A tenderly factual film about two asthmatics who find happiness in an Arizona trailor camp on an oxygen tank built for two.

★★★★★★★★★★★★★★★★★★★★★★★★★★
CHOKING
★★★★★★★★★★★★★★★★★★★★★★★★★★

Discussed are the pros and cons of choking, the use of black gloves around your head nurse's throat, and the technique of "simulated strangulation" to fend off amorous residents. Also demonstrated are various methods to rescue choking victims, from the popular Heimlich maneuver to the not-so-popular window-ledge technique.

★★★★★★★★★★★★★★★★★★★★★★★★★★
AT LAST, THE EBP
★★★★★★★★★★★★★★★★★★★★★★★★★★

A full course on the brand new Electric Bedpan (EBP). How and where to plug it in, how it eliminates germs by infrared lighting and doubles as a bed-warmer. Learn how a faulty fuse can blow it and feces to pieces.

★★★★★★★★★★★★★★★★★★★★★★★★★★
THE INOCULATOR
★★★★★★★★★★★★★★★★★★★★★★★★★★

You've seen *The Terminator*. Now it's time for *The Inoculator,* a nursing suspense thriller that will have you on pins and needles. *The Inoculator* is a nurse with a mission to boldly seek out the arms and cheeks of new victims and stick it to them.

★★★★★★★★★★★★★★★★★★★★★★★★★★
GAY MEANS MORE THAN CHEERFUL
★★★★★★★★★★★★★★★★★★★★★★★★★★

This film explains how to communicate more effectively with gay patients. How to intercept bedside passes from members of your own sex and say no to occasional requests for unnecessary enemas.

★★★★★★★★★★★★★★★★★★★★★★★★★★
THAT'S VD
★★★★★★★★★★★★★★★★★★★★★★★★★★

This nostalgic flick includes classic uncut scenes from some of the great VD films of the last thirty years. You'll laugh, you'll cry, you'll burn—but you'll remember those good old days.

****

NEW TECHNIQUES FOR TREATING VICTIMS OF BOBSLEDDING ACCIDENTS

****

Most people don't realize that more people are injured in bobsledding accidents every year than are injured by having six-packs of Diet Pepsi fall from the refrigerator onto their feet. How to set broken bones through snow and give injections through layers of thermal underwear are featured.

****

COMING ATTRACTIONS

****

Tracheotomy: Fun, or a pain in the neck?
Invasion of the Body Scratchers: How to treat a rash of rashes.
Back to the Butcher: A senile former surgeon returns to work and disrupts the course of medical history.

What Is Burnout?

The time may arise in your nursing career when your white uniform will start turning gray. This is a sign that one of the following has occurred:

1. Your eyesight is going.
2. You forgot to add bleach to your wash load.

3. You joined the Confederate Army.
4. You're suffering from burnout.

burnout: 1. To stop burning from lack of fuel. 2. To wear out or become inoperative as a result of heat or friction. 3. To become exhausted, especially as a result of overwork or dissipation.

Sometimes you'll get a second wind, but quite often burnout means you may have chosen the wrong career and are now ready for another one. Some of the professions ex-nurses have switched to and excelled at are: floral arrangement, TV repair, housecleaning, and massage parlor work.

Fifteen Ways to Tell if Burnout Has Set In

1. Every time you make a bed, you find yourself irresistibly drawn to lie down on it for a while.
2. You start putting quarters in EKG monitors, thinking they are video games.
3. Your sick days outnumber your work days.
4. You start putting straws in specimen cups and distributing them to patients.
5. You begin giving serious thought to a career as an Amway distributor.
6. You order a pizza for the operating room.

7. You apply for a transfer to *St. Elsewhere*.

8. You order second portions in the hospital cafeteria.

9. You begin paying serious attention to the ads that say, "If you can draw this, you could be a professional artist."

10. You wear your uniform to the market and not only squeeze the fruit but check a papaya for a pulse.

11. You walk around attached to a portable IV filled with black coffee.

12. You play tic-tac-toe with other burned-out nurses on patients' charts.

13. You wear black lace stockings instead of white support hose.

14. You let visitors stay in the patients' rooms into the wee hours and party with them.

15. The patients start pushing *you* around in the wheelchairs.

CHAPTER SIX

The Personal Nurse

Dealing with the Off-Duty Nurse

Nurses, like everyone else, pick up habits from their jobs and bring them into their everyday lives. For example, if you know a nurse who spends twenty-five minutes washing up for dinner, boils her sheets and drapes, and sets the table with thirteen different types of utensils, chances are you're dealing with a surgical nurse. Should a smoke alarm, TV test pattern, or apartment buzzer system send a nurse into a panic, you may be dealing with an ICU nurse. Pediatric nurses can be spotted moving slowly past Toys 'R' Us stores and often opt for jigsaw over crossword puzzles. Or say you've invited a friend and some of your relatives over for dinner, and your friend sees them one at a time; you may be playing host to a nurse who works in a doctor's office.

Nobody said knowing a nurse, or living with one, wouldn't be interesting. Nurses deal with a wide range of people and problems on a daily basis and they always have stories to tell. In fact, if you're living with a nurse who's had a hard day, don't even think of falling asleep until she has had a chance to describe her day to you in detail. Always feel free to nudge a nurse you know well if her story about the botulism outbreak on the ward doesn't fit in with the dinner table conversation. And if you take a nurse out for dinner, be prepared to remind her not to cut your meat into bite-sized pieces.

As the saying goes, "You can take the nurse out of the hospital, but you can't always take the hospital out of the nurse. "But it could be worse—you could be living with or dating a doctor."

Sex and the Single Nurse

There are quite a number of males who seem to think that

"nurse" is a synonym for "nympho" and that the traits that add up to the letters *R.N.* on-duty stand for something quite different off-duty, such as Really Naughty or Red-hot Number.

It's true that nurses are "giving" people, who live to make others comfortable and give them "relief." They also deal with the human body, inside and out, on a much more intimate basis than most of us. These features, coupled with their pristine white uniforms, create an irresistible "virgin-vixen" allure to both the single and the not-so-single male. Add to this the sordid tales of doctors and nurses making it in broom closets, empty beds, and even the deserted O.R., and you have the fantasy (or reality) of "the sensuous nurse."

As far as the notion of the nurse as an uncontrollable sex maniac on the job, stop to think about it. Hospital apparel, that worn by patients and personnel alike, is far from attractive, never mind erotically stimulating. And the hospital itself, with its antiseptic scent and sterile decor, is not exactly conducive to romantic interludes. Nor are bedpans, IVs and the various bodily functions and fluids of sick people aphrodisiac in nature. As for the nudity a nurse is exposed to during the course of her workday, 60 percent looks like the "before" photo in an ad for a drastic health regimen,

while another 30 percent is more wrinkled than most sheets.

If the truth be told, outside the hospital is where most nurses do their mingling, matching, and mating—but first comes meeting. Letting on to a date that you're a nurse is not necessary, but if it should be made known, you're automatically assumed to be able to give a great massage and to know more about a male's body than he does. Your job lends itself nicely both to encouraging and to discouraging male advances. Stamina, versatility, your need to "let go," and the fact that you're a night person can act as come-ons—while graphic descriptions of surgery, gory incidents in the E.R., accidents involving bedpans and bleeding, or the fact that you're far too overtired to put in any "overtime" tonight can work quite well as deterrents.

If you're involved romantically with a nurse, bear in mind that most R.N.'s especially enjoy good food and leisurely meals in fine restaurants. Also, you should get creative with gifts, since a nurse's first reaction to flowers or candy is that they're not meant for her.

As for after-hours activities, it isn't actually true that nurses prefer white bedsheets and tucked-in corners even in motel rooms; nor do they check their lover's vital signs during foreplay. And while it is true that nurses are very clean and prefer their partners to be the same, it's a myth that they chart their partner's performance. Finally, while there are probably a few nurses around who are into kinky sex, most of them get to vent such urges on the job with the use of restraints and side rails.

To a nurse's sexual advantage, she usually has a lot of stamina, and in case her lover doesn't, she is well-trained in CPR!

How to Socialize with a Doctor

Some nurses simply can't get enough of doctors. If you're a nurse who has actually chosen to spend some free time with an M.D., here are some conversation tips that will keep the ball, and perhaps the relationship, rolling.

1. Talk about his patients—that is, the survivors.
2. Talk about his hobbies, even if they're somewhat bizarre, such as collecting antique crutches, touring cemeteries, or the secret lives of bacteria.
3. Talk about his family, especially Mom.
4. Talk about his days at medical school and those hilarious pranks and practical jokes that'll have you "on the floor"—trying to crawl away unnoticed.
5. Talk about golf, especially in terms of the great courses

they have on Caribbean islands.
6. Ignore numbers 1 through 5, since your doctor date will talk about himself all night anyway.
7. Forget about "socializing" with a doctor.

How to Live with a Doctor

If, by some bizarre twist of fate, your attempts to socialize with a doctor have led to something more serious, here are a few tips on how to hack it on the home front.

1. "Take orders" about household matters, then ignore them.
2. Have a stiff drink or two before visiting his folks.
3. After the wedding, plan separate social activities, since you'll probably never run into each other again.
4. Buy him a sex manual. Buy yourself sex toys.

Medical Mating

Getting Personal with Hospital Personnel

Besides doctors and nurses, interns and residents, orderlies and aides, there are some other types of possible mating material wandering around the hospital or other medical facility where you work. In case you haven't noticed, we're listing some of them here.

PATIENTS

Sometimes you don't just want to make them well—you want to make them, period. Keep in mind that too much T.L.C. (Tender Loving Care) could result in a Touchy Legal Contest. So mind your bedside manners, at least until your charges are discharged.

PHARMACISTS

They're usually honest, but suspicious, because they think people are only after them for drugs. They're probably right. But watch out, because R_x could also mean Rated X!

X-RAY TECHNICIANS

These hip young people are generally found hanging out in hospital corridors, boogeying to the funky beat issuing from their huge transistor radios. They sought this particular profession for a wide range of ulterior motives—some to score drugs, some to score with candy stripers, and others simply to see people naked. Remember, X-ray can also mean X-rated.

MEDICAL JOURNALISTS

These sensation-seekers pal around with the medical community, speak the jargon, and always greet you by name. They can be charismatic and will often wine and dine you in pursuit of a juicy "story." Be careful about crawling under the covers with them—or you might find yourself on the cover of a trashy tabloid.

CANDY STRIPERS

They're bright-eyed, fresh-faced, and curvaceous in their cute little pinafores, and flirtatious, too. But before you date 'em, bear in mind that J.B. (Just Beautiful) can also stand for Jail Bait.

SOCIAL WORKERS

If you're into lectures on the woes of urban blight and poverty, these people will oblige. They're caring and giving, but they also tend to be humorless and sometimes seriously depressed. If you want a heavy-duty relationship instead of a frivolous fling, give one of them a whirl. But bear in mind that S.W. (Social Worker) can also stand for Serious Wimp and Social Waste.

Nurses on Call

R.N.'s Telephone Answering Machine Messages

"Hi, this is Rosie and I'm not at home at the moment. In fact, I'm hardly ever home. You could make a futile attempt to reach me at the hospital, but the odds of them tracking me down are about fifty to one. If you'd like, you can leave a message after the beep, but the way my schedule is, please don't hold it against me if I can't call you back for a month or two. Thanks for calling anyway."

* * *

"Hi, this is Nancy and I can't come to the phone right now. Please leave a message after the beep. Tell me who is calling, how we are feeling today, if we slept well, if we're hungry, and if there's anything else we need. Hope we are comfy, and do ring again if you want anything, okay?"

* * *

"Hi, this is Beth, and I'm sleeping. No, Mom, I can't come over and take your blood pressure again today. No, Uncle Max, I don't know anything about hair transplants. No, Aunt Phyllis, I didn't get a chance to ask Dr. Roth about your wart. After all, it was our first date. No, Cousin Ralphie, I can't get you drugs. Please leave a message after the beep-tone if you have any further medical questions."

Tuning In to RNTV

The Nurse's Favorite Cable TV Channel

7:00   I Dream of Nursing
A nurse pops out of a magic IV bottle and makes her male patient healthy again—so healthy, in fact, that he becomes an oil magnate on *Dallas*.

7:30   Hogan's Nurses
A team of World War II nurse-spies infiltrate a German army base, feeding hospital food to SS soldiers and forcing them to listen to lectures on dental hygiene until they crack up.

8:00   Hospital Gown Junction
Fevers rise and pulses race when a hospital ward of young male patients invades a female ward full of nose job and breast-implant patients.

8:30   Julia
Diahann Carroll stars as the multifaceted minority sweetheart of nursing, proving that only in America can a black single parent progress from regis-

tered nurse to *Dynasty* millionairess.

9:00 Maureen Welby, R.N.
Roberta Young, a visiting nurse famous for her friendly bedside manner, makes housecalls and chats with patients, curing not only their physical ills, but their mental, emotional, family, and financial problems as well.

9:30 Nursing Feud
Nurses from different hospitals kiss and kibitz with Richard Dawson, then battle it out for big bucks by naming the most popular diseases, operations, painkillers, malpractice suits, and much, much more.

10:00 M*A*S*H*E*D
A group of zany Army nurses and doctors drink, mess around, crack sick jokes, and poison the enemy with deadly hospital mashed potatoes.

10:30 The Queer Couple
Can a tough, macho hocky player with filthy personal habits, and a finicky, immaculate male nurse live together without maiming or killing each other?

11:00 The Six-Million-Dollar Nurse
A supernurse constructed from donated organs, artificial limbs, tubes, bandages, and hospital bed parts solves crimes and baffling medical cases while dating every handsome doctor in sight.

WATCH FOR THESE OTHER RNTV FAVORITES

Little Hospital on the Prairie
Nursing for Dollars
The Hill Street Whites
The N-Team
Flo and Clara
Lifestyles of the Underpaid and Exhausted

As we come to the end of our all-too-brief look at the world of the saint—er, nurse—it is only fitting that the music come to a rising crescendo. Hit it:

Nurses' Favorite Songs
The R.N.'s Hit Parade

"Ain't No Sunshine (on This Shift)"

"Dedicated to the Job I Love"

"Dirty Laundry"

"Doctor My Eyes" (and Nurse the Rest of Me)

"Does Anybody Really Know What Time It Is?"

"Easier Said Than Done" (An Ode to Nursing)

"Eight Days a Week" (An Ode to Scheduling)

"Everybody's Talkin' " (An Ode to Visiting Hours)

"Goin' Out of My Head"

"Hard Day's Night"

"Hold on, I'm Comin' " (An Ode to Call Lights)

"How Can You Mend a Broken Heart?"

"Hush" (An Ode to Pediatrics)

"I Could Have Worked All Night"

"I Don't Need No Doctor"

"I Only Have IVs for You"

"(Intra) Venus"

"Just Dropped in to See What Condition My Condition Was in"

"Land of 1,000 Patients"

"Long Cool Woman in a White Dress"

"Mack the Knife" (An Ode to Surgical Nursing)

"Needles and Pins"

"Never Been to Spain" (An Ode to Vacations)

"19th Nervous Breakdown"

"Nurse in White Satin"

"Nurse with No Name" (An Ode to Name Tags)

"Psychotic Reaction" (An Ode to Psychiatric Nursing)

"Shout (Some Days They Make Me Wanna . . .)"

"Sixteen Tons" (An Ode to Lifting Patients)

"So You Wanna be a Hospital Star"

"Take This Job and Shove It"

"Whiter Shade of Pale"

"Yackety Yak (Don't Talk Back)"

 And finally,

"You'll Never Walk Alone" (An Ode to Walkers)

QUESTION: What's the difference between a resuscitation doll and a famous psychiatrist?
ANSWER: The first is full of cool air; the second is full of hot air.

"MY MOM'S A NURSE": Common Responses Your Kids Will Get

1. "Is she on *General Hospital?*"
2. "Does she give out free lollipops?"
3. "Does she see a lot of dead people?"
4. "Yuck!"
5. "I'll bet she makes you take medicine all the time!"
6. "Can she get us some real blood for Halloween?"
7. "Really? Is your dad a doctor?"